TOWARDS A NEW LIBERATION THEOLOGY:

REFLECTIONS ON
PALESTINE

Edited by Arzu Merali and Javad Sharbaf

Islamic Human Rights Commission

www.ihrc.org.uk

2009
PUBLISHED BY
ISLAMIC HUMAN RIGHTS COMMISSION

First published in Great Britain in 2009
by Islamic Human Rights Commission
PO Box 598, Wembley, HA9 7XH
© 2009 Islamic Human Rights Commission
Design & Typeset: Ibrahim Sadikovic
Cover photo: Nir Landau/Activestills.org

ISBN 978-1-903718-346

Contents

Acknowledgements

The editors would like to thank: Aisha Abbasi, Musthak Ahmed, Selina Akhtar, Abdulnasser Baston, Abidah Merchant, Raza Kazim, George Robertson, Massoud Shadjareh, Jon Catherall, Barirah Limbada, Faisal Bodi, Samira Quraishy, Sara Khorshid, Sheikh Saeed Bahmanpour, Imam Muhammad al-Asi, Professor Saied Reza Ameli, Imam Achmad Cassiem, Rabbi Ahron Cohen, May Sobhi El-Khansa, Rima Fakhry, Archimandrite Attalla Hanna, Barirah Limbada, Fr. Joe McVeigh, Dr. Ilan Pappe, Dr. Ghada Ramahi, Dr Javad Sharbaf, Rev. Stephen Sizer, Leah Tsemel, Rabbi Yisroel Weiss, Mohammed Nasrin Nasir, Beena Faridi, Amir Zaidi, Shazia Ramzan, Sadia Ramzan, Sabiha Hanif, Sofia Dewji, Sanjida Akhter, Fahad Ansari, Muhammad Dharas, Seyfeddin Kara, Fatemeh Rezavie and Muhammad Kamali.

Notes on Contributors & Editors

Imam Muhammad Al-Asi is a Research Fellow of the Institute of Contemporary Islamic Thought (www.islamicthought.org). He is also the elected Imam of the Islamic Centre in Washington DC and an advisor to the Islamic Human Rights Commission. He is a well-known Islamic scholar and has recently completed an exegesis of the Holy Qur'an.

Professor Saied Reza Ameli is a professor of sociology and mass communications and is the Director of the Institute for North American and European Studies at the University of Tehran and assistant professor for Media and Cultural Studies in the Faculty of Social Sciences. He is also a member of the international committee of the Global Studies Association, UK. He is an honorary research fellow in the Department of American and Canadian Studies, University of Birmingham. He is one of the founders of the Islamic Human rights Commission.

Imam Achmad Cassiem is the Chair of the Islamic Unity Convention, an umbrella body for over 250 organisations in South Africa. Imam Achmad Cassiem is a well-known figure from the anti-apartheid struggle and spent a total of 11 years imprisoned during the apartheid era, 9 of which he spent on Robben Island. He has held various senior positions in the Pan African Congress, including that of Secretary-General. He is an advisor to the Islamic Human Rights Commission.

Rabbi Ahron Cohen is a member of Neturei Karta; a group actively involved in spreading the message regarding the absolute opposition to Zionism held by authentic Orthodox Jewry. Rabbi Cohen stresses that Judaism and Zionism are totally different concepts and are in fact diametrically opposed. He is one of many Orthodox Jews who sympathise with the cause of the Palestinians in their struggle against the Zionist State.

May Sobhi El-Khansa holds a B.A. in law from the Lebanese University in 1984-1985, and is awaiting her PHD from the international law from the American university. Amongst her many positions she has been a member of Beirut Bar Association since 1985; she is Chair of the Philantrophic Association of Rehabilitation; a participating member of the Arab Lawyers' Union (ALU); an activist in all issues related to Human Rights and other modern cases; a member of the World Media Association - Universal Human Rights; and a member of the Amnesty International; a member of the ASF (Avocats Sans Frontieres). She is also the first person to bring a lawsuit against the Israeli leadership for the massacres perpetrated against the Lebanese and the Palestinian people, concerning their displacement and the violation of their lands, and calling for the return of the refugees to their homelands before the Lebanese and the Spanish judiciary. She is the author of *Return Back is a Right*, published in 2004 (in Arabic), and *The Birth of the Foundling*, published in 2007. She is also the chair of association "Marsad" for Human Rights in Beirut.

Rima Fakhry is a Lebanese activist based in Beirut. She is a member of the political council of Hizbullah. An agricultural engineer by profession, she has been active in the educational field particularly that is related with Muslim women in Lebanon. She has a keen interest in social and political studies, and has been vociferous in her opposition to the Israeli occupation of South Lebanon that ended in 2000. She continues her political activism in Lebanon today.

Archimandrite Attalla Hanna is the spokesman of the Greek Orthodox Patriarchate, based in Jerusalem. Born in 1965, he was ordained in 1991 and has courted controversy with his statements calling for joint Christian & Muslim action against Israeli forces, as well as being part of the procedure that saw George W. Bush, Tony Blair, Donald Rumsfeld and Jack Straw banned from the Church of the Nativity and excommunicated in 2003.

Barirah Limbada graduated in Modern History & Politics from the School of Oriental & African Studies (SOAS), University of London. Her particular areas of academic interests are identity politics, more specifically ethnic, national and political identities as well as the socio-political and legal development of Islam.

Fr. Joe McVeigh is from Fermanagh, Ireland and is the author of *A Wounded Church: Religion, Politics and Justice in Ireland* (1989) , *Renewing the Irish Church: Towards and Irish Liberation Theology* (1993) and *Crying Out for Justice* (1997). Ordained in 1971, Fr. McVeigh has been active in his opposition to British involvement in Ireland and Irish affairs. He has suffered persecution by British security forces and disapproval from the hierarchy of the Irish church. Father McVeigh has studied Conflict Resolution and works with the Belfast Human Rights Centre. He is editor of 'Irish Witness'.

Arzu Merali heads the research section at the Islamic Human Rights Commission (www.ihrc.org.uk) and is one of its founders. She is a writer on human rights issues and is based in London, UK. She is also editor in chief of Palestine Internationalist (www.palint.org). Her academic background includes English Literature, Law and International Relations, and has studied at Cambridge University, Nottingham Trent University and the University of Kent.

Dr. Ilan Pappe was a senior lecturer of Political Science at Haifa University at the time of the conference and the Academic Director of the Research Institute for Peace at Givat Haviva. He is currently a professor of History at the University of Exeter, UK. His recent books include *The Making of the Arab-Israeli Conflict, 1948-1951*(1992), *The Israel\Palestine Question* (1999*). A History of Modern Palestine* (2003*)* and *The Modern Middle East* (2005). Dr. Pappe is a member of the Advisory Board of the Council for Palestinian Restitution and Repatriation (CPRR); an organization which declares that "every Palestinian has a legitimate, individual right to return to his or her original home and to absolute restitution of his or her property."

Dr. Ghada Ramahi is Palestinian born and received her formal education in the USA. Upon finishing her Ph.D. training in molecular genetics and virology, she realized that Western science is neither "objective" or value-free, rather it is highly subjective and used for political agendas. Her teaching and research interests include: multicultural perspectives on science and technology; History and Philosophy of Western and non-Western sciences as well as technology and society.

Dr Javad Sharbaf was born in 1969 in Mashad, Iran. He studied political science at Tarbiat Moddares University and Tehran University from where he received his masters degree and Ph.D. He has written many articles and books including *Persian Gulf and Related Issues; Israeli Militarism and Its Effects on Middle East.* He is currently a professor at Tehran Azad University.

Rev. Stephen Sizer is a well known and respected activist on issues surrounding Palestine. He is vice-chairman of Highway Projects, a Christian charity sending teams of young people to serve the indigenous Church in the Holy Land. He is a member of Anglican Mainstream, a Trustee of the Amos Trust, on the Advisory Board of the Friends of Sabeel UK, which supports the Sabeel Ecumenical Theology Centre in Jerusalem. Rev. Sizer is also on the UK Board of Reference for the Mar Elias Educational Institutions, Ibillin, in Galilee founded by Elias Chacour.

Leah Tsemel was born in Haifa in 1945. She is an Israeli lawyer who is active in the representation of Palestinian political prisoners. She has advocated on various human rights issues, in particular children's rights. She has become better known for her defence of failed suicide / martyr bombers, famously stating in a BBC interview, "I grew up on the myth of better suicide than surrender. So what is so special about suicide bombers?"

Rabbi Yisroel Weiss is the spokesperson for Neturei Karta; the anti-Zionist orthodox Jewish Movement. He is based in Brooklyn and has campaigned vigorously against the occupation of the Holy Land. Rabbi Weiss was one of the three rabbis from Neturei Karta that joined IHRC's team at the World Conference Against Racism in 2001 in Durban, South Africa. During this trip he publicly embraced the father of 12 year old Mohammed Al-Durra, who was murdered by Israeli soldiers in 2000 at the start of the second intifada.

Foreword

In June 2005, the Islamic Human Rights Commission and NEDA convened a conference of academics, theologians and practitioners entitled 'Towards a New Liberation Theology: Reflections on Palestine' the papers submitted for which form the content of this book.

The conference was intended to be the first in a series of events and books exploring the relationship between the practical experiences of those living through events in various world flashpoints, their faith affiliations and aspirations and the possibilities of effecting justice through their goals rather than the imposition of 'peace' at any price and without any relevance to those it would most affect. Put more simply, this is an exercise in realizing the potential that religion has in resolving conflicts that have been irresolvable through secular initiatives.

The contents of this volume reflect contributors' responses to the conference title and range from polemical, jurisprudential, sociological through to esoterical. Based on experiences in the Holy Land and beyond, including Lebanon, Ireland, Central and South America, and South Africa, this book articulates the religious challenge to oppression and injustice in the context of the Palestinian struggle for justice.

It is the editors' hope that the importance that faith plays in the lives of those whose everyday experience is oppression and whose religious beliefs form part of their hope for transformation, be taken seriously by policy makers and peace brokers. Anything else would be undemocratic. Anything else would be disempowering and not liberatory for those without power and effective representation. Anything else would simply be a perpetuation of the festering and violent injustices that characterize the current conflict in the Middle East.

Islamic Human Rights Commission and NEDA

Introduction

Palestine, Liberation and Theology

Arzu Merali and Barirah Limbada

Conceptualising the Palestinian struggle has taken many forms. Whilst political fora have focused on secular narratives as a partner in negotiations in the form of a variety of left-wing and nationalistic ideologies associated with the PLO and associated organisations. Despite decades of rejection, eventually the international community and even Israeli authorities sought and found hands to hold in this politicisation of Palestinian struggle.

Running contemporaneously, but often portrayed as contrary to these movements is a religiously driven set of narratives associated initially with Islamic Jihad and since the first intifada, Hamas. Religion in the Palestinian context, popularly understood and institutionally conveyed, is Islam. In this oft-cited view, it is Islam as opposed to Judaism that is thought to define not only the national narrative of the Israeli state but its raison d'etre and its legitimacy. Leaving aside the implications of the demonisation of one religion and sanctification of another within this simplistic vision of politics, nationhood and faith, this book sets out the views of those from religious traditions of resistance, within and without the Palestinian context in order to bring to light the anomalies and normativity of secular and religious struggle.

The papers – all written before the election of the Hamas government in the Palestinian territories, look not at why religion in a politicised sense is important to the Palestinian masses, but why its importance can and should be understood as a universal cry for justice and freedom that should inform the political process.

The editors of this volume are conscious of the many views of Liberation Theology, within a Christian context as well the revisiting of this concept within and beyond the Christian tradition with reference to gender, geography and confession. Further work that brings together theorists, theologians and practitioners is already in motion to take forward the ideas and discussion raised by the 2005 conference. This volume sets out (a) polemical stall(s), but it does not conform to one ideological or confessional stance, nor do its contributions speak from within one discipline. Using the idea of Liberation Theology as a way to re-conceptualise ideas around faith, religion, struggle and politics, the papers look at existing examples of this form of Christology as well as moot its limitations within and without Palestine and includes visions of what it could and perhaps already means from different faith perspectives and none. Amongst the key themes that this raised, justice and oppression as derived through theological concepts and praxis were illuminated through the traditions of Islam, Christianity and Judaism, in Palestine but also historically from South and

Central America, South Africa and Northern Ireland. Set out in the opening speech of the conference was the idea of the chosen People as a religious concept. The elevated position of the oppressed confirms their status as the chosen people of God regardless of their confessional or ethnic background. The universality of this concept realigns theological concepts and practice across confessional boundaries and undermines any tendency to exceptionalism that internally focussed discourses on religion can tend to.

Whilst theological claims to Holy Land arise, the vista for conflict is repeatedly laid beyond that door. Concerns such as the denial of self-determination and continued occupation invoke the right to resistance as a form of justice. Clearly there is much diversity in the types of resistance invoked and justified and papers in this volume discuss the validity of both armed and unarmed resistance, using recent praxis and sociological and theological arguments to argue for and against guerrilla wars, the military intervention of states, pacifistic but active resistance in the form of economic boycotts and creating parallel economic structures, to awareness raising.

The porosity of political and national boundaries in the current age of globalisation is also invoked as a practical tool for the opposition to oppression but also as a virtual ground for the emergence of a new global consciousness – the next step in solidarity with the oppressed in Palestine and beyond.

Four themes were repeatedly raised and discussed amongst the papers. A subtle difference in emphasis is evident on the purpose and project of Zionism. Ameli, McVeigh, Casseim, and El-Khansa understand Zionism to be a project of (neo)-colonialism, emphasising temporal issues of self-determination of a collective. Whereas Weiss and Cohen understand the character of Zionism to be unjust and misguided but simultaneously emphasise that Zionism is a direct challenge to providence and the divine decree of exile as well as a stain on Judaism, thus highlighting and stressing doctrinal and spiritual matters. Al-Asi shifts the emphasis again to argue that the true custodians of Palestine are those concerned about and possessed with justice.

The right to resist injustice characterises these papers. Implicit in Ameli's paper is the notion that resistances and opposition to oppression is a benign religious duty stemming from religious dictates of justice and fairness. Ramahi understands resistance as a divinely decreed right (haq). Cassiem suggests that resistance is the law of nature. It is clear from reading these texts and throughout the collection that these positions are not mutually exclusive.

As regards, the methods of resistance, Ameli sees the virtual world as the social space in which resistance and opposition to oppression can emerge, inclusive of resistance to Zionism and support for Palestine opposition. Pappe argues that the education system is an important and useful tool in defeating the ideological foundations of Zionism and the ensuing Islamophobia that informs Israeli culture. There exists a tension relating to armed and unarmed resistance, exemplified in the examples given by Sizer of the Sabeel-Palestinian Liberation Theology Centre as opposed to Cassiem and Ramahi's exposition of the inherent right to armed resistance. These tensions are also hinted at in the examples cited by Joe McVeigh.

Apparent too is an implicit difference of opinion on the role of the international community and its effectiveness. Ameli suggests that justice can be implemented or enhanced when "communities without states" begin to emerge; when individuals are able and willing to make judgements outside of the prevalent socio- political norms of their given societies. Implicit in this position is the view that organised state structures and, by extension, the international political system inherently privileges national interest (just or unjust) over and above justice, hence the need for 'communities without states'. On the other hand, Pappe calls for 'imposing of sanctions on Israel like those tha twere imposed on South Africa'. He further argues that 'the UN and Britain have particular responsibility for forcing Israel.... to allow the Palestinian refugees to return'.

Pappe extends an effective role and responsibility to states and collective international state structures. In highlighting the failure to implement UN resolutions regarding the right to Palestinian refugees to return, El-Khansa implicitly assumes and accepts the role of the international community but highlights its ineffective.

The relevance of theology lies in the values of equity, justice, truth and compassion for the weak and vulnerable, that are present in all major faiths. The aforementioned virtues are not limited to one's own faith community; rather these are virtues that one should apply to all of humanity. As Ameli states, all are equal to one and one is equal to all.

The scriptural dictates for the pursuit of justice and the injunction against oppression are quoted from all three represented traditions. In the historical analyses of these papers, Liberation Theology implies an active pursuit of justice and active resistance to oppression, and is seen as playing an effective role in reshaping the societies of Latin America and was instrumental in the fight against apartheid in South Africa. Acknowledging the normativity of faith in the struggle against oppression has happened in these contexts. Liberation Theology has overcome the stigma and demonisaion attached to it by its detractors within and without established churches. Its normalisation is one that needs to be emulated with regards to the understanding of other religious contexts of struggle. The current attempts to decry all religious affiliation in politics as variously archaic and barbaric is not only unjust oversimplification, but anathema to the recent history of religion and struggle. The editors hope that this volume contextualises religion in the Palestinian – Israeli conflict within that recent history, and helps posit the idea of faith as part of the solution and not the problems of the region.

PART ONE

Why a New Liberation Theology?

This section presents the keynote paper of the conference by Saied R. Ameli and the papers of Joe McVeigh and Ilan Pappe which include responses to some of the themes raised by Ameli.

Contained within these discussions are an overview of what Liberation Theology is generally understood to mean i.e. in a specifically Christian context (Ameli); the experiences of a practitioner (McVeigh) the limitations of that understanding (McVeigh) and the universalisation of the concept of justice and equality borne out of faith discourses on liberation, in particular Islam and Christianity (Ameli and McVeigh); and the idea of the oppressed as God's chosen people without distinction as to faith.

The practical aspects of how this theology is and can be lived out within the Palestinian context is further discussed. Ameli suggests that justice can be implemented or enhanced when "communities without states" begin to emerge; when individuals are able and willing to make judgements outside of the prevalent socio- political norms of their given societies. Implicit in this position is the view that organised state structures and by extension the international political system inherently privileges national interest (just or unjust) over and above justice, hence the need for 'communities without states'.

McVeigh highlights the role of Liberation Theology in Ireland and the move towards mainstreaming Republican aspirations against a British military presence in the North. He also draws on inspirations from his own experience and readings relating to Central and South America. He sees the ideas expressed in Liberation Theology as bringing a new dynamic into situations of conflict by taking away fear of legalised authority. This has inspired the organisation of base church communities to speak out against injustice.

Pappe advocates educational reform and innovation to defeat the ideological underpinnings of Zionism and the ensuing Islamophobia that characterizes Israeli society. He further calls for the imposition of sanctions on Israel like those imposed on South Africa. He contends that states and collective international state structures have an effective role and responsibility, and argues that the UN and Britain have particular responsibility for forcing Israel to allow the Palestinian refugees to return.

Universality of Liberation Theology: One is Equal to All and All are Equal to One

Saied R. Ameli

Department of Communications & Institute for North American and European Studies – University of Tehran

Abstract

Liberation Theology: Theology of movement and resistance
LT emerges when theology is isolated form public life and when people are isolated from the products of religion leading to a nostalgia for justice and metaphysical values.

LT requires three major elements to work as a universal force applicable to, among other things, solving the Palestinian problem:

Return to God: Foster the concept of universality of God. Variety of insular God communities detracts from universal message of mercy, compassion and commitment to the poor and oppressed, as these attributes are understood to be applicable to one's specific God community.
Selflessness: Minimization of personal desires & dogmatic attachment to nationality, ethnicity and even religion is central to caring of the oppressed.
Centrality of Justice: Decentralisation of ethnicity and centralization of Justice. This position advocates the liberation of Palestine. Justice is the point of engagement between religion and politics.

Palestine has become a symbolic icon of oppression, deprivation and injustice.
Occupation of Palestine is an important global issue which should properly be understood as neo-colonialism.

Globalisation is the social ground for the emergence of Universal Values.
Emergence of Second World/Virtual World gives instant opportunities for resistance and support for opposition to oppression.

That is why we decreed for the Children of Israel that whoever kills a soul, without (being guilty of) manslaughter or corruption on the earth, is as though he had killed all mankind, and whoever saves a life is as though he had saved all mankind... (Surat Al-Maidah, Versus 32)

Introduction

Palestine and resistance are two interconnected central terms in discussing liberation movements in our age. Liberation theology is a theory which can explain why the resistance movement in Palestine is important and why people of the world gradually feel responsible about Palestinian oppressed society.

Liberation theology is a theology of movement and resistance (Jeanrond, 1992). In contrast 'civil theology', marked the parameters of a conversation or debate which rested on the shared assumption that there was some correlation between a society's religion and its government (Kidd, 1999:1010). Liberation theology was an attempt for liberation of the people from poverty and oppression. It was also a desecularization action for reinforcing politics in the social aspect of religion. Liberation theology can also be defined as a religious resistance in response to socialist and Marxist liberation theory which extensively influenced Latin American society in Nicaragua, Brazil and Chile. However, liberation theology in the Christian world was considered as a leftist approach to God and Society (Dodson, 1979). Generally speaking churches are not primarily intended to function as political movements but as spiritual agencies (Levine, 1989). The most effective limit upon their political capacity is the resistance of members to excessive political entanglement (Wald et al, 1988: 534). The issue of religion and politics reflects the question posed by Marx and Weber: Can traditional religious institutions be agents of change in an evolving society (Silvert, 1967 and Smith, 1975)?

Nevertheless, the social and political context created a serious challenge for religious institutions that showed them as being detached from political and social reality. Therefore, in response to both theoretical and practical demands, the Latin American movements appeared to be the solution. Liberation theology is a revolutionary vision which for many theologians in the Christian world was considered a rebellion, corruption and wrong interpretation of religion. This was because according to the Catholic doctrine, which dominates the religious institutions of Latin America, religion and politics/political power should not coincide. But the church in Latin America came to the stage that either it would lose all followers of the faith and leave the ground to Marxism or it should undertake some serious action for the support of the poor and oppressed people. Therefore, it can be argued that liberation theology was a 'determinative choice' for the Church.

Within oppressed societies, the sociology of Liberation is also a conscious raising theory. It is perhaps more than merely a conscious raising, which has moved the sociology of liberation to an activist type of work rather than an academic discipline of thought. That activity is not on behalf of the oppressed, rather, it is achieved through learning to see the world from the perspective of the oppressed and joining with them, adding sociological theories and methods and data to their anti-establishment arsenal. In the case under discussion, liberation sociology is joining the Palestinian homeless and the Palestinians who have lost their children, fathers and mothers, so as to understand what homelessness in your own home means (Deutscher, 2002).

The power of liberation theology returns to its compassion for the poor and its conviction that the Christian should not remain passive or indifferent to the plight of the poor or oppressed. According to liberation theology, religion can not be neutral even if it is secular. Religion exists to give a safe life and to save people from any deprivation and life disturbance. Religion has to solve individual as well as social problems and it should be dynamic and open to touch all social and political problems. However, from a sociological perspective, liberation theory is a response to public demand; the demand for justice and liberation from all injustice. It was not only a demand in a particular place, since the emergence of liberation theology has become a unique and permanent political movement throughout Latin America; from Mexico to Chile, from Nicaragua to Brazil, this movement has been politically effective in merging together traditional, religious values with a commitment to social activism on behalf of the "poor and Oppressed" (Pottenger, 1989).

Liberation theologians believe that the orthodox doctrine of God tends to manipulate God in favour of the capitalistic social structure. They claim that orthodoxy has been dependent upon ancient Greek notions of God which perceive God as a static being who is distant and removed from human history. These distorted notions of God's transcendence and majesty have resulted in a theology which thinks of God as "up there" or "out there." Consequently the majority of Latin Americans have become passive in the face of injustice and superstitious in their religiosity. Liberation theology responds by stressing the incomprehensible mysteriousness of the reality of God. God cannot be summarized in objectifying language or known through a list of doctrines. God is found in the course of human history. God is not a perfect, immutable entity, "squatting outside the world". He stands before us on the frontier of the historical future. God is the driving force of history causing the Christian to experience transcendence as a "permanent cultural revolution". Suffering and pain become the motivating force for knowing God. The God of the future is the crucified God who submerges himself in a world of misery. God is found on the crosses of the oppressed rather than in beauty, power, or wisdom.

In this paper the conceptual aspect of Liberation Theology together with its contextual background will be discussed in an attempt to answer to two major questions: firstly, is this theory, as a leftist Christian theology which claims to have been initiated in Latin America, applicable to a global problem such as 'global poverty' and the "Palestinian Liberation Movement" as global and local issues. And secondly, how liberation theology can be reconstructed, so that it can solve 'global and local problems', despite it's affiliation to a particular religion, race or ethnicity. In other words, how liberation theology can become a universal force for solving the clashes, conflicts, poverty and deprivation today.

Background to the Concept

Many state that the start 'liberation theology' was from the emergence of the Latin American Liberation Movement in which Latin American pastors confronted in the latter half of 20th century the reality that most of their parishioners lived in grinding, abject poverty — and that the Church represented the only viable community organization in their world. Out of this awareness came a new understanding of the very meaning of the Church's work. The movement that came to be called "Liberation Theology" began with the awareness that it is blasphemous to care for people's souls while ignoring their needs for food, shelter and human dignity. As Jesus participated in the suffering of the poor, and proclaimed to them the good news of justice and freedom, so must today's church engage in the struggle for justice in *this* world (Gutierrez, 1973 and 1974, Greenberg, 2000 and C. Boff and L. Boff, 2004).

For this group, liberation theology and images that immediately come to mind are those of 1960s-style antiwar, anti-establishment priests like the Berrigan brothers or, more recently, Bishop Samuel Ruiz García with his obvious sympathy with the downtrodden Indians and Zapatista rebels in Chiapas. Many social scientists try to monopolize liberation theology into a Marxist theory of class and dependence. For example Dodson (1979:206) stated that the 'clergy radicalized by direct involvement with the poor required tools for explaining the social relationships they encountered, and for justifying some form of political action to ameliorate those conditions'. Hence, liberation theology evolved as an amalgam of Marxist social analysis and reinterpretation of the prophetic tradition in Christianity.' For Jim Tuck (2005) Liberation theology didn't begin with the Berrigan brothers or Bishop Ruiz, but it goes back to the 15th and 16th centuries. A remarkable man, Las Casas devoted the greater part of his 92 years on earth to ameliorating the lives of non-Caucasian people who lived in the vast Spanish empire. First known as a protector of Indians, he also became an advocate of black Africans who had been brought over by the Spaniards as slaves.

Liberation theology puzzled many academic theologians. In the formal theological sense, it rejected many tenets of European and North American liberal theology, both Catholic and Protestant, because they had accommodated the social and political assumptions of imperialism and bourgeois culture. As Gutiérrez put it, while liberal theology sought to speak to nonbelievers and saw its challenge as the skeptical "modern mind," liberation theology addressed itself to "nonpersons".

According to Cox (2005) three coexisting social, religious and philosophical changes caused the emergence of liberation theology in Latin America. First the worsening social and economic conditions for the majority of people in Latin America in the 1950s created a desire and expectations for change. Secondly, the structural causes of poverty were addressed in Latin American dependency theory, and class-based inequities were identified in Marxist critiques of capitalist systems. By the late 1950s a revolutionary climate was apparent in the region, exemplified by the Cuban Revolution of 1959. The third important macro change comes through the Second Vatican Council (1962-1965). Pope John XXIII opened the council by expressing the hope that the Catholic Church "might become once again…the church of the poor". Then in 1968 the Conference of Latin American Bishops (Consejo Episcopal Latino Americano, or CELAM) held the Second General Conference of Latin American Bishops in Medellín, Colombia, where the bishops discussed how to apply the Vatican Council's resolutions within their own troubled communities. Among the theological advisers to the bishops was a Peruvian priest, Gustavo Gutiérrez, who had worked in the poorest sections of Lima, Peru. His thinking substantially shaped the Medellín document, which became the manifesto of the liberation theology movement (Cox, 2005).

Typology of Liberation Theology

It is generally agreed that liberation theology encompasses three overlapping levels (L. Boff & C. Boff, 2004):

1) Professional Level: carried out by scholars schooled in the language and tradition of Christian reflection.

2) Pastoral level: concerned with the proper strategies for Christian ministry in a world of poverty and oppression.

3) Popular level: generally expressed in oral or folk traditions, which centres on worship and festivals as ways to nurture human life under difficult circumstances.

According to Universal liberation theology the fourth type which is related to the popular level of liberation theology is the 'Global Network and Popular Movement'. This type of liberation theology is about people's involvement in the construction of justice and caring for the poor. The Global level of liberation theology, while arising from divine religions, is not manipulated by a particular faith group. Muslims, Christians and Jews stand for liberation of the poor and oppressed peoples because this is the most recommended principal in all divine faiths. They care about oppression, because for them oppressed societies are the only chosen societies for which everybody should feel responsible. From this angle, the oppressed people are the poor creatures of God, for whom everybody - no matter what faith they are, have an affiliation to and by consequence should care about. Here the paradigm of 'one is equal to all and all are equal to one' is extensively alive, therefore their sympathy is related to every single oppressed person in the world. Sometimes they react globally for a single person who has been discriminated against tragically; sometimes they stand for the rights of the collectively deprived such as the isolated, homeless refugees of Palestine, its children and civilians, who do not have any instrument of defence except stones.

Opposition to Liberation Theology

Many of the opponents of Liberation theology claim that the Latin American Theology of Liberation is widely assumed to be too Marxist. However for Kee (1990) it is not Marxist enough. It is continuously criticized for its unquestioned acceptance of Marx.

Criticism of liberation theology began immediately after the 1968 Medellín conference. The movement was growing rapidly, but conservative forces within the Latin American church tried to stem the tide. More traditional Catholic thinkers accused it of being unduly dependent on Marxism and Vatican authorities and conservative bishops criticized the base communities as a dangerous parallel church outside the hierarchy of papal authority (Cox, 2005).

Meanwhile, liberal theologians, both Catholic and Protestant, accused the movement of ideological bias and thin scholarship. Feminists, blacks, and some indigenous leaders criticized it for emphasizing economic forms of oppression at the expense of gender, racial, and ethnic discrimination. Even feminist theology which is committed to the struggle for justice for women and the transformation of society, considered it critical that the theology of liberation engaged in the reconstruction of theology and religion in the service of this transformation process, in the specificity of the many contexts in which women live (Grey, 2004: 89). The liberation theologians themselves responded vigorously to these criticisms, wrote hundreds of books and articles, and made liberation theology one of the most provocative and original progressive movements of the second half of the century (Cox, 2005).

When the bishops' council of Latin America convened for its Third General Conference in 1979 in Puebla, Mexico, opponents within the Church were determined to issue a stern warning against the movement and condemn the base communities outright. They did not succeed, however, as bishops sympathetic to the movement prevailed. Nothing was said about liberation theology in the final document, and base communities were actually endorsed. Nevertheless, Pope John Paul II, while issuing statements in support of the poor, clearly signalled that he disapproved of a people's church and of liberation theology. One by one, bishops who supported base communities were replaced upon their retirement by churchmen antagonistic to them (Cox, 2005).

However, the opposition mounted by military regimes and paramilitary death squads was more crushing. Authoritarian governments feared the critical ideas of liberation theology and the activism of the base communities, especially after the Nicaraguan Sandinistas, who were directly influenced by liberation theology, successfully overthrew their country's dictatorship in 1979. Priests, nuns, and catechists were arrested, tortured, and murdered throughout Latin America. The most vicious repression occurred in El Salvador, during the country's civil war from 1979 to 1992. In March 1980 a paramilitary death squad assassinated Archbishop Romero, one of El Salvador's most outspoken critics of the government and a respected figure, while he was conducting a church service. Then national guardsmen raped and murdered four American women—three nuns and a lay worker—in December of that year, attracting further international attention to the violence in El Salvador. Liberation theologians themselves also came under attack: In November 1989 an army unit invaded the Jesuit-run Central American University of José Simeón Cañas, where such noted liberation theologians as Ignacio Ellacuria and Jon Sobrino taught and wrote, and murdered six of the Jesuits as well as their housekeeper and her daughter.

Other factors reshaped liberation theology as well. The replacement of military regimes by civilian governments in Latin America meant that community churches were no longer the sole bases for opposition. Unions, universities, political parties, and social movements began to play that role as well. In addition, criticisms by Latin American feminist theologians such as Ivone Gebara in Brazil and by black theologians such as James Cone forced the largely male and white liberation theologians to reconsider their lack of emphasis on gender and race. The spectacular growth of Pentecostal Christianity in the 1980s and 1990s made many Latin American liberationists wonder if their approach had been too political and analytical and not sufficiently spiritual and emotional. Meanwhile, the Vatican under Pope John Paul II actively resisted secularization in the Church and opposed direct political participation by priests (Cox, 2005).

At the same time, however, liberation theology began to flourish in other regions of the world and in other religions. Books and articles developing Jewish, Buddhist, and Muslim liberation theologies appeared. In South Korea during the 1970s and 1980s a movement developed, largely under Latin American influence, called *minjung* theology (Korean for "ordinary people"). In Germany, when the pastors who led the nonviolent marches in Leipzig that contributed to the toppling of the Berlin Wall in 1989 were asked about what had influenced them, they mentioned Martin Luther King Jr., the German resistance pastor Dietrich Bonhoeffer, and Latin American liberation theology. In the United States, Roman Catholic bishops issued their pastoral letter on the economy, "Economic Justice for All," which explicitly credited the Latin American church for contributing the preferential option for the poor to their thinking. Bishop Desmond Tutu and other religious leaders in South Africa were also inspired in part by the movement, and a specifically black South African school of biblical interpretation has emerged in scholarly works such as Itumeleng J. Mosala's *Biblical Hermeneutics and Black Theology in South Africa* (1989). More recently, Asian liberation theologian Tissa Balasuriya's *Mary and Human Liberation* (1997) drew sharp criticism from the Vatican, and Balasuriya was for a time excommunicated for his views (Cox, 2005).

In Latin America and the Caribbean, some observers have suggested that liberation theology is in decline. Another, and perhaps more accurate, view is that it is going through a period of transition, enlarging and refining its perspectives and continuing to influence similar movements in many parts of the world. *See also* Black Theology in Latin America and the Caribbean: An Interpretation (Cox, 2005).

Two Nostalgias: Loss of Justice and God

The important question is why did liberation theology emerge? The answer is related to the characteristics of theological approach in the academic sphere and within religious institutions such as the Church and missionary schools. Theology gradually became a clerical debate abstract from ordinary life because of two significant isolations: isolation of theology from public life and every day life and isolated people from the social products of religion. These two isolations arose from two interrelated social contexts; the first is the result of the frustration of social and political spaces resulting from a useless and selfish interference of the Church in the arena of power and the second is the result of a wrong understanding of religion.

Isolation of religion from public life and politics turned religion into a historical context which turned out 'museum types of ideas'. On the other hand religion - particularly in the process of secularization - lost its power in significant aspects of social life and one can further argue that religion lost its cultural influence. Therefore, it seems to me that Liberation theology is a response towards two important local and global nostalgias; the first and the most important one is nostalgia for justice and the second one is nostalgia of metaphysical values, both of which are universal values and have strong potential for turning any social action into universal practice. However the universality of any social and political values requires popularity among masses. Universal values that are recommended through all divine messages in the past, reversely converted to local and community values can convince logically and prudently every single member of human society in the World..

Universality of Liberation Theology

Liberation theology requires three major elements to work as a universal force, and hence be applicable in solving the Palestinian problem and other 'global and collective problems' which are related to oppressed society even if they have different religions and belong to different national and ethnic groups:

1) **Return to God**: we are all fair from God whether we are Muslims, Christians or Jews; if we are not fair to God, we cannot be fair to ourselves and we cannot be fair to others. To liberate Palestinians, one needs to see them as creatures of the same God and one needs to see them as members of their own community. To do this other followers of faith must be liberated from, and force 'the International Community' to liberate (the idea of) God from any 'Chosen Community' attachment. The only Chosen People are the oppressed and the poor. This is why today, Palestinians should be considered 'The Chosen Oppressed Community'.

> The Return to God has two important aspects:
> 1) We need to give serious attention to the existence of God and that we will encounter our Lord. This will affect our practice on the earth with ourselves and with others: "So whoever expects to encounter his Lord, let him act righteously, and not associate anyone with the worship of his Lord (Surah Al-Kahf, Versus, 110)."
> 2) The universality of the perception of God. The perception of God has been fragmented into many Gods; Muslims, Jews and Christians and other religions divided God metaphorically to a variety of 'God's communities' which effectively means, "My God is different to your God." This is indeed affects consciously and unconsciously our relationship with other creatures of God. As a result the universality of mercifulness, the universality of sympathy and commitment to the pain of the people becomes dependent on whether we consider them as a member of 'God's community' or not. According to all divine messages there is no difference between people except by their level of closeness to God:

"O mankind! Indeed We created you from a male and female, and made you nations and tribes that you may identity with one another. Indeed the noblest of you in the sight of Allah is the most Godwary among you. Indeed Allah is all-knowing, all-aware" (Al-Hujarat, versus 13).

While in the age of globalization, the trend for 'endness' has become the 'archetype' for the presentation of all 'new ideas', it seems society needs and expresses a desire for a return to human origin to purify all impurities have come to dominate the life.

One of these 'returns' is the return to an involvement of religion in politics. Liberation theology was considered as a turning point for the repoliticization of religion and an act towards the desecularization of politics (Levine, 1990:229). While the first amendment to the constitution of America was emphasized that 'Congress shall make no law respecting an establishment of religion, or prohibiting the free exercise thereof' (Kidd, 1999:1007), this amendment became the source for much conflict and objections among clerics such as Thomas Curry and other conservatives. Social situations also helped wither the expansion of religion's role in society. However, it was not possible to draw a precise line between religion, politics, culture and economics.

2) **Selflessness:** Selflessness, the minimization of *personal desires* and dogmatic attachments to nationality, ethnicity and even religion is a major requirement for caring for the oppressed and poor people. This entails avoiding all those considered as 'selfish'. 'Self' here is not only a person, but it can cover all 'collective centralities' such as Eurocentrism, Americocentrism and Zionism, which ultimately require the demolishing and destruction of 'others' for the price of supporting the 'self'. Selflessness is a divine and mystical soul in all divine religions which brings God's spirit to all aspects of life. Consequently, such ambition motivates one's 'caring' tendencies, and even the sacrificing of life for 'others', rather than dominating, marginalizing, torturing and executing 'others'. Here is the position where the Palestinian problem becomes a global issue for all human beings who care about 'others', here is the position at which 'all become equal to one and one becomes equal to all'; here is the position at which one can observe unity within diversity and diversity within unity.

Berofsky (1995:236) argues "that the self is formed through interactions with others". It depends on what is our understanding about ourselves and what is our understanding about others. Those who see 'self' and 'others' in the same level of existence without making any priority and advantage for a particular gender group, race or even religious group, affects their social vision and their social practice.

3) **Centrality of Justice:** Decentralization of ethnicity and centralization of Justice for all human beings is another major element for the empowerment of the 'Universality of Liberation Theology'. Here is the position which advocates the

sociological approach to the liberation of Palestinian. According to Christianity equality is not to admit either individualism or collectivism, for it is an equality of dignity which excludes the slavery of some or of all which involves the notion of the equality of men (Drummond, 1955:2).

In the Islamic concept, 'justice' is used in contrast to 'selfishness' or 'sinful desire'. That is why Imam Ali articulated that 'justice is enthusiastic and selfish desires destructive'. According to Imam Ali, 'Justice is the master force for all human rights[ii], without justice all religious orders are meaningless. He is also emphasizing that 'the core of life is justice'[iii].

Justice is about power and it is indeed the point of engagement which interlinked religion and politics. The relationship between power and the Church or Islam and Politics is at the core of many important researches and historical challenges in the past (Misztal & Shupe, 1992, Percy, 1998).

Chosen Society is Oppressed Society - US and Others

The Universality of liberation theology needs a strong 'priority social system' which motivates people towards support for all oppressed and needy people. The priority social system is usually activated by ethnicity, race, religion and in many cases has arisen through affiliation to power. Zionist Jews consider themselves as a chosen people who should dominate all over the world, not only in the economic and political arena but also geographically. This priority system will cause risk to lives and trouble for the rest of the world. Such motivation can create serious clashes and even war in a global context.

Theology gradually became a clerical debate abstract from ordinary life: and it created dual isolations; isolation of theology from public life and isolation of people from the social products of religion. These two isolations convey that religion had become manipulated in a historical context and its ideas outdated rather than expressing practical social and political values. Liberation theology is a reverse attempt to incorporate religion as a practical aspect of life in social and political directions. According to Christian principles, Liberation theology's emphasis upon the poor gives the impression that the poor are not only the object of God's concern but the salvific and revelatory subject. Only the cry of the oppressed is the voice of God. Everything else is projected as a vain attempt to comprehend God by some self-serving means. This is a confused and misleading notion. Biblical theology reveals that God is for the poor, but it does not teach that the poor are the actual embodiment of God in today's world. Liberation theology threatens to politicize the gospel to the point that the poor are offered a solution that could be provided with or without Jesus Christ.

In Islamic theology, respect and support to the poor is also a positive value and it is indeed a privileged principle. Prophet Mohammad addressed that: Indeed God supports this community because of the prayer, worship and purity of the weak[iv].

Prophet Mohammad said: Shall I let you know about the kings of the Heaven? Every powerless deprived[v]. According to Islam the future is in the hand of those who have been kept powerless and deprived. It is articulated in the Holy Book that: And We desired to show favour to those who were deprived in the land, and to make them Imams, and to make them the inheritors[vi]. On the other hand, oppression is considered as the most damaging sin. Oppression is significantly destructive because first of all it is a social phenomenon and secondly it caused deprivation, marginalization and muting of the voice of people. Oppression becomes constructively damaging when it happens against those who are alone, poor and without any support. Imam Ali said: Oppressing the poor is the worst oppression[vii]. For Imam Ali, oppression was considered as the mother of all sins[viii]. He also emphasises that 'Oppression is a destructive force'[ix].

According to universal liberation theology, distinctive boundaries between 'us' and 'others' are symbolically related to the concepts of justice and injustice. 'Us' is globally inclusive and extends so that all people of the world can be considered as insiders and members of the family of 'truth'. Us is exclusive only when it comes to oppressors; those who individually or collectively destroy the 'right of the people'. According to Islamic liberation theology, in this respect 'one is equal to all and all are equal to one'. There is no difference between males and females, black and white, poor and rich. Injustice is dreadful no matter whether it takes place against a Muslim, Christian or even those who don't believe in God. Injustice is destructive no matter whether it is turned against poor or rich and other factors such as nationality, race, gender, social position and anything related to man's status is meaningless. That is why from a theological perspective particularly divine theology and in more articulated expression Islamic Theology, the only particularity that exists if that of an 'oppressed society'. They are the chosen society that demands sympathy and the motivation of liberation from the people.

Applicability of Universal Liberation Theology to Palestine

Colonialism and the occupation of the land by force are regarded as the most painful deprivation and marginalization. It was a political tradition in Europe that to the extent a European state has power, it should overwhelm other territory. That is why in the 1930s, following almost five centuries of European overseas imperialist expansion, colonies and ex-colonies covered about 85 per cent of the land surface of the globe. No wonder such a historical and geographical sweep makes summaries impossible and the theorisation of the formation of colonialism—namely, how the political, economic and cultural systems of Europe overpowered overseas territories—disputable. The nature of colonialism varied enormously within and among different European empires in different times (Dixon and Heffernan, 1991; Loomba, 1998). Occupation of Palestine was the result of an ideological Zionist global domination which was stimulated by the British colonialist experience. For nearly 50 years the Anglo-Jewish community sent mixed signals to successive British governments about the land of Palestine as an ideal land for the Anglo-Jewish community (Zakeim, 1999).

The occupation of Palestine overtly and covertly is an important global issue because it works as a gateway for new colonialism during a period of decolonialisation; it should be seen as neocolonialism by force and military action.

Palestine has become the symbolic central icon for oppression, deprivation and injustice. People of the land, deported unjustly with violence and force have become homeless without any recompense. The Palestinian refugees total 18% of the all refugees world-wide.

Proportion of Palestinian Refugees Compared to Rest of the World

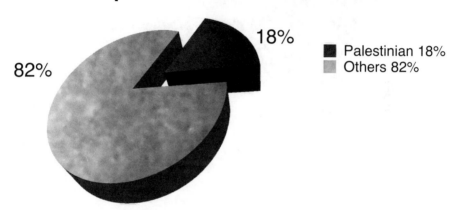

According to Universal liberation theology with particular emphasis on contextual ground, one can articulate the role of globalization on the applicability of liberation approach in the global context. We are living in the age of globalization. Globalization has instrument life for the universality of truth; it is indeed a ground for the emergence of 'universal values'. Globalization is about more connectivity, more velocity and meaninglessness of time and place. This means, it does not matter where you are, if you are liberated or looking for liberation of all abandoned, neglected and oppressed people then you can be with them; your hand can be with Palestinians regardless of whether you are physically in Palestine or you are far away from the land of resistance. Everywhere is Palestine and all people of the world can feel membership of the community of Palestinians.

Emergence of the second world i.e. the Virtual World, gives an instant opportunity for resistance, for mobilizing support and for opposition to oppression. Liberation Theology here means feeling free from all hesitation which caused the 'fragmentation of truth' and it gives global ground for campaigning for justice for all.

The trend of people who have lost their home and their motherland of Palestine are significantly proliferated. According to UN data, the number of refugees exploded from 870,158 in 1953 to 4,255,126 in 2005. This means that in another 50 years will Palestine become completely a land of non-Palestinians.

Number of Palestinian Refugees

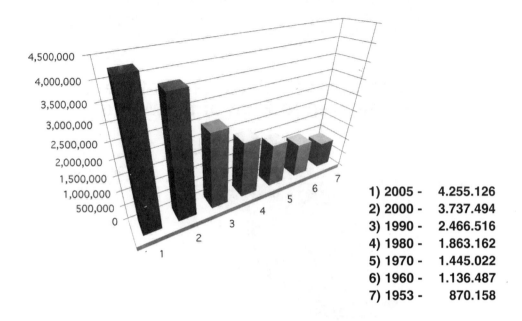

1) 2005 -	4.255.126
2) 2000 -	3.737.494
3) 1990 -	2.466.516
4) 1980 -	1.863.162
5) 1970 -	1.445.022
6) 1960 -	1.136.487
7) 1953 -	870.158

Palestine is not only a tragic example of homelessness, but it sadly also exemplifies poverty, life insecurity and health-insecurity and food-insecurity. Levels of food insecurity in the occupied Palestinian territory (OPT) are high. Over a million Palestinians are food-insecure, and another 975,000 are at risk of becoming so. This food insecurity is caused primarily by Israel's closure policy and movement restrictions, which have resulted in massive increases in unemployment and underemployment (up to 30% in the West Bank and 40% in the Gaza Strip). **(Source: Humanitarian Practice Network).**

This was a short review of the catastrophic story of Palestine, the agony and pain of which throughout the last fifty years has become constructively damaging without any serious improvement in coming to a resolution. Palestine is a land of disastrous effects on all age groups, males and females, infants and elders, infirm and disabled. Homelessness and lack of food can be seen a problem for a 'collective oppressed nation' which potentially can affect 'all human beings'. Therefore if one looks at the problem from the perspective of liberation theology, the extent of oppression, the level of poverty and multiplicity of tragedy can affect ordinary lives of people in the world. Therefore it is right to say Palestine is a 'millennium dome' (Ameli, 2003). It is an indicator of the global pain and global challenges for human rights and human life.

Conclusion

According to Universal Liberation Theology, the issue of Palestine cannot come to any positive end unless world society collectively moves to change the situation. It seems there is a positive sign for overcoming the pain and injustice in the solidarity of people in contrast to the 'arena of power'—political and economical authoritative power which looks for domination over people's lives in both the cultural and political arenas.

According to liberation theology, injustice is the master force for all pains and troubles in human society. Injustice is the main reason for all the distinctions between 'us' and 'others'. Here we need to emphasis three central points:

1. Centrality of 'self' or 'community' or even a particular race, nation and faith is the main cause for all local and global challenges and it is indeed the most significant example of injustice in a social aspect of life. Here self not only reflects one person, but it can also explain a collective ideology/identity. Selfcentrism, community-centrism and ethnocentrism are major forces for all 'injustice' at an individual level and social level. The tragedy of Palestine is the result of racism, religio-centrism and community-centrism i.e. Zionism. Universal liberation theology's emphasis in contrast is on 'God-centrism' and decentralization of 'self', 'community', nation and even particular 'faith'. From the view point of Islam, 'selflessness' is a central source of the establishment of 'justice for all' and reinforcement of the paradigm of 'one is equal to all and all are equal to one'. In a wider context, community centrism is an epistemological reason for the emergence of Americanism, Eurocentrism, Zionism and all selfishness which is the main cause for mass destruction of human society. Therefore, human rights should not only concentrate on individual and objective cases, but it should emphasise the social context which subjectively causes the destruction of 'others'. If the genocide of Palestinian children increases enormously and the number of refugees extensively explodes, if Palestinians are under serious life threat because of food and health and we don't observe a serious reaction, these are all the price of the 'culture of self-centrism and community-centrism'. The culture of self-centrism and community-centrism is a precise example of social discrimination and it is indeed a social example for anti-human rights action. In such a culture, the oppressed people of Palestine can easily be ignored. In such an environment, the poor children of Palestine, because of being Palestinian and not being for example European or American can be ignored as happened in the mass destruction in Iraq in comparison to what happened on September 11th. The viewpoint of universal liberation theology is that life is important no matter whose life it is, because all are equal in terms of 'life right'.
2. Social injustice and social discrimination against individuals and nations is the main cause for the extension of global challenges. In other words social discrimination against an individual creates a 'reaction potential' for social discrimination against collective members of a society. Therefore as a part of

'global conflict resolution', a wise society should think of demolishing injustice in all aspects and at all levels. It seems world power will not have any more win-win situations, as a powerful country can stand for war and genocide, individuals and small groups can cause risk for human life and the interests of power. This is a very dangerous phenomenon, which can threaten order, security, peace and trust in the human society.

3. Globalization played an important role in reinforcing 'individuality'. Individuality here means one who sees, thinks and decides personally despite the dominated social, political and economic norms of the society. Here the concept of mass industry and mass culture is under serious question. Empowerment of individuality gradually resulted in the emergence of a 'community without state', a community that in relation to 'oppressed society' feels responsibility. As a result of this detachment from a collective ideological attachment such as racism, and nationalism, one can observe its reaction in the actions of the masses against injustice all around the world. For this community boundaries between 'us' and 'others' become meaningless. All oppressed no matter what nationality, religious order or social group they belong to, are considered as the 'home community'. Therefore they react and they stand for their rights. Here, extensive sympathy is and will be observable for support of Palestinian and all oppressed peoples in the Muslim, Christian and Jewish world. This sympathy is even applicable to those oppressed people all around the world who do not believe in any particular divine religion.

Here one can be hopeful that through construction of a universal liberation theology, pain and oppression can be reduced or else, an optimistic impression may disappear from human society. Caring becomes the central motivation beyond any gender, racial, national and religious boundaries for people of the world. Here, one could be hopeful in seeing the replacement of 'self' and 'community' centrism by the implementation of a 'common message' of all divine religions which stands for the 'reduction or demolishing of pain' from human life and giving more attention to 'poor society' and 'oppressed people.'

Bibliography

Ameli, S. R. (2003) Semiotic Understanding of Palestinian Movements versus Global Exceptionalism: Euro-centrism and Americo-centrism, present in International Conference on Jerusalem/Al-Quds: The City of Three Monotheistic Faiths and Islamic Role. Paper is available in www.ihrc.org.

Berofsky, B. (1995) Liberation from Self: A Theory of Personal Autonomy, Cambridge, Cambridge University Press.

Boff, L. & Boff, C. (2004) Introducing Liberal Theology, Maryknoll & New York, Orbis Books.

Cox, H. (2005) Liberation Theology in Latin America and the Caribbean, Encarta Reference Library Premium.

Deutscher, I. (2002) Gazing at the Disciplinary Bellybutton: A Review Essay on Liberation Sociology, Contemporary Sociology, Vol. 31(4), pp. 379-382.

Dixon, C. and Heffernan, M. (Eds) (1991) Colonialism and Development in the Contemporary World. London: Mansell.

Dodson, M. (1979) Liberation Theology and Christian Radicalism in Contemporary Latin America, Journal of Latin American Studies, Vol. 11 (1), pp. 203-222.

Drummond, W. F. (1955) Social Justice, USA, The Bruce Publishing Company.

Greenberg, A. (2000) The Church and the revitalization of politics and community, Political Science Quarterly, Vol. 115 (3): 377–394.

Grey, M. (2004) Feminist Theology: A Critical Theology of Liberation, in C. Rowland (ed.), The Cambridge Companion to Liberation Theology, Cambridge, Cambridge University Press.

Gutierrez, G. (1973) A Theology of Liberation, Maryknoll, New York, Orbis Books.

Gutierrez, G. (1974) Liberation theology and the proclamation, in Claude Geffre and Gustavo Gutierrez(eds.), The Mystical and Political Dimension of the Gospel, Concilium Series 96. NewYork, Herder and Herder.

Kee, A. (1990) Marx and the Failure of Liberation Theology, London, SCM Press.

Kidd, C. (1999) Civil Theology and Church Establishments in Revolutionary America, The Historical Journal, Vol. 42(4), pp. 1007-1026.

Jeanrond, W. G. (1992) From Resistance to Liberation Theology: German Theologians and the Non/Resistance to the National Socialist Regime, The Journal of Modern History, Vol. 64, pp. 187-203.

Levine, D. H. (1986) Is Religion Being Politicized? And Other Pressing Questions Latin America Poses, Vol. 19(4), pp. 825-831.

Levine, D. H. (1990) How Not to Understand Liberation Theology, Nicaragua or Both, Journal of Interamerican Studies and World affairs, Vol. 32(3), pp. 229-245.

Loomba, A. (1998) Colonialism/Postcolonialism. London: Routledge. Misztal, B. & Shupe, A. eds. (1992) Religion and Politics in Comparative Perspective: Review of Religious Fundamentalism in East and West, London, Praeger Publisher.

Percy, M. (1998) Power and the Church, Ecclesiology in an Age of Transition, London and Washington, Cassell.

Pottenger, J. R. (1989) The Political Theory of Liberation Theology: Towards a Reconvergence of Social Values and Social Science, New York, State University of New York Press.

Silvert, K. (1967) Churches and States: the Religious Institution and Modernization New York, American Universities Field .

Smith, B. (1978) The Catholic Church and Political Change in Chile, 1925-1975, PhD Dissertation, Yale University.

Tuck, J. (2005) Bartolome De Las Casas: Father Of Liberation Theology. (1474 - 1566), Mexico Connect

Wald, K. D., Owen, D. E. & Hill, S. S. (1988) Churches as Political Communities, in The Amrican Political Science Review, Vol. 82(2), pp. 531-548.

Zakheim, D. S. (1999) The British Reaction to Zionism: 1895 to the 1990s, The Round Table, No. 350, pp. 321-332.

End Notes:

[i] Quran: Al-Hujurat, Verse 13
[ii] Gorar-al-hekam, 386
[iii] Gorar-al-hekam, 247
[iv] Al-Doro-al-mansor, 724/2.
[v] Kanzol-ommal, 5943.
[vi] Quran, Qasas, verse 5
[vii] Nahjul-Balagheh, Book 31
[viii] Gorar-al-hekam, 804
[ix] Gorar-al-hekam, 6

Liberation Theology and The Palestinian Struggle for Self Determination

Joe McVeigh

Belfast Human Rights Centre and editor of 'Irish Witness', Ireland

Abstract

Liberation Theology focuses on injustice and the liberation of the oppressed. The statement that the chosen people are the oppressed people sums up what liberation theology for the Palestinian people can be about.

Faith in the God of Justice and Truth, faith in the God of the Oppressed has been important to many involved in the Irish struggle. Critical to faith is stand witness to justice, to stand in solidarity with the oppressed and not in solidarity to a particular group or nationality. Faith impels and compels us to work unceasingly for justice and freedom- a real justice that is empowering. Faith should always compel us to be self-critical and self-aware especially when we have attained out political ambition and/or political power.

As a Catholic Priest and Human Rights Activist I have been inspired by the writings of Liberation theologians and the re-reading of the scripture.

Ideas expressed in LT brings new dynamic into situations of conflict. LT takes away fear of legalised authority.

The supposition of a tribal or nationalistic concept of divine election is no longer theologically defensible. Divine partiality is contextual, not exclusive or related to one ethnic group.

All three faiths are called to address their religious and nationalistic exclusivism and to listen to a God of Justice whose Oneness transcends and overcomes all religious and ethnic divisions.

Introduction

At first I was reluctant to speak at this conference. There are too many pitfalls -I told myself. I am not well informed about your situation. I have only ever visited your land once -and that was about thirty years ago when I was a rather naive tourist/pilgrim. I was reluctant to speak here because I have always been a bit suspicious of outsiders -especially clergymen -who came to speak in Ireland about our situation. It used to annoy me when some people came from the United States or England to tell us how terrible it was that Protestants and Catholics could not live together and that what we needed was to learn to be more tolerant and to create better community relations -like more coffee mornings attended by Catholics and Protestants! This view was based on the mistaken notion that our conflict was about religion and religious intolerance. That was the British propaganda version. Many of these speakers bought into that propaganda. It is the basis of what we call the Community Relations Industry -one of the main industries left in Belfast.

There was no reference by many of these outsiders to the occupation and the aggression of the British, the collusion with pro-British death squads, the dirty tricks of MI 5 setting up counter-terrorist groups and organising assassinations; no talk of the undercover work of the British military establishment nor of the long history of colonialism and repression. Most of these outside commentators always turned a blind eye to the long history of colonial occupation and the denial of the Irish peoples right to self-determination.

I am aware that the Palestinian people have had to endure the same kind of propaganda and bias in the media as we have had to endure. The point is well made by John Pilger: With honourable exceptions, events in Palestine are reported in the West in terms of two warring rivals, not as the oppression of an illegal occupier and the resistance of the occupied. The Israeli regime continues to set the international news agenda. Israelis are murdered by terrorists, while Palestinians are left dead after a clash with security forces (John Pilger, The New Rulers of the World p139).

I agreed to talk here when I saw that the Conference was focused on Liberation Theology -because I believe that Liberation Theology can cut through a lot of the nonsense and superficial talk about community relations. For with Liberation Theology the focus is on injustice and the liberation of the oppressed.

The Palestinian Struggle and The Irish Struggle

The Palestinian people have much in common with the oppressed Irish. The Palestinian people like the Irish have been dispossessed and suffered because of British colonial rule. There is, as a result, a strong sense of solidarity among Irish republicans with the Palestinian people.

Of course, those who consider themselves the elect or the chosen peoplein our situation in Ireland -Mr Paisley and the Orange order -identify with the Israeli Zionists. They fly the flag of the Israelis on certain occasions -as during the Ardoyne/Glenbryn school protest. They believe in the God of the elect so as well as the middle of the road Christians those of us seeking liberation had to contend with right wing zealots associated with Paisley's Free Presbyterian church and other Fundamentalist groups like the Orange order.

Christian Fundamentalism

Paisley has much in common with those right wing Christian fundamentalists in the US. In a new book, The Last Crusade by Barbara Victor, the author shows how the Christian Right has grown in the USA to become a great ally of Zionism and an enemy of the Palestinian cause. The Religious Right -Christian and Zionist are a real threat to world peace today. This group has much influence in the US where it represents over 20 per cent of voters and played a big part in putting Bush into power.

As well as being a religion of sorts Christian Fundamentalism in the US has a very clear political agenda -not just in the States but with regard to the Middle East. These people are opposed to the Palestinians having their own state and are intent in holding this back but they will not succeed.

A Liberation Theology

The subject we are here to discuss is the possibility of a Liberation theology for the Palestinian people. That is to say: How can religious faith help in the struggle for freedom, justice and truth in Palestine?

The statement that the chosen people are the oppressed people sums up what a Liberation Theology for Palestine could be about.

I want to share with you something about OUR experience in Ireland and how a few of us found Liberation Theology of help in theory and in practice. (I have also seen at first hand and heard and read about the resilience of many people in Central and South America faced with economic and military oppression. Many of my friends are working there as Missionaries alongside the poorest of the poor. They tell me about the political advances that are being made in spite of tremendous obstacles. It is their faith in the God of Justice and Truth that encouraged them to keep going with this work and with the struggle for justice).

For many involved in the struggle in Ireland it is our Faith in the God of Justice and Truth, the God of the Oppressed, which has supported us down through many years of suffering and sorrow. There are others who have found courage and strength from other sources.

If our faith is based on the Word of God, then we will want to witness to the God of the Oppressed. It seems to me that the thing that is critical about faith is the witness to justice (witnessing justice in solidarity with the oppressed -not with any nationality or particular group). That is why our faith is nourished by the witness of great martyrs and great prophets and by our own witness to what is true. It is that faith that impels us and compels us to work incessantly for justice and freedom -a real justice that is empowering- that gives people hope for themselves and their children. It is a Faith that will continue to be witness to Justice even when political change takes place and the people achieve some of their political goals. It is a Faith that is always self-critical and self-aware of the call to witness to justice and truth -even should we attain power and especially when we attain power.

In all of my work as a Catholic priest and human rights activist over the years, I have been inspired by the writings of Liberation Theologians and by re-reading of the Scriptures -especially the Prophets and the Gospels from the viewpoint of the oppressed.

The writings of some Liberation Theologians from South and Central America and perhaps especially those from South Africa were available to us in the early 1970s and I found them truly inspiring. I was most inspired by the Kairos Documents which were published in 1988 and the writings of Albert Nolan, a priest of the Dominican order (who once when asked to become the head of his Religious Order refused and said it was easy to be a Pope –it was more difficult to be a priest standing with the poor and oppressed).

The Kairos Statements offered a very critical view of official Church theology and State theology -the kind of theology that sacralises the status quo and denounces the people who would cry out for freedom. I found the ideas and words in the Kairos statements and also the conversations published by Nicaraguan Ernesto Cardenal in the Gospel of Solentiname to be truly powerful and inspiring. How inspiring must these reflections have been for the people and for those Church based groups and Christians in South Africa seeking justice when there was so much hostility and so much opposition to their struggle from their own government and some churchmen and from governments around the world.

But as well as the writings and reflections of these remarkable and courageous people, I was also inspired by the example and witness of certain leaders and priests and catechists and community leaders, people like Monsenor Oscar Romero in El Salvador, Helder Camara, Cardinal Arns, the Boffs in Brazil, the Cardenals in Nicaragua, and all those wonderful people in El Salvador etc (I had the great joy to visit there some years ago).

I joined in the campaigns for justice in my home country because I wanted to show solidarity with those who were working for Justice and Human rights at home, some of whom risked their lives. There has always been in recent years in the Church in Ireland, support for people fighting for justice faraway. We call it long -distance Christianity...it was easy... to be concerned about people in Nicaragua etc but it was a different ball game, taking up the cause of the people in the six counties.

It soon became apparent to me how similar our struggle was to the Palestinian struggle and to other struggles in South Africa and El Salvador...it was always about the poor and the poorest of the poor achieving justice. The connections with other struggles became most obvious to me during my time in the US between 1980 and 1983.

When I came back from the US in 1983, I joined in a number of different justice campaigns. I also began to document the cases of harassment and intimidation of my parishioners and my neighbours. I sought publicity for the people being harassed. I learned the importance of this from a man called Bill Wifler at the NCC in New York. He was a human rights activist in Chile and Argentina. When I came back from the US in 1983, we set about taking statements and making official complaints. This brought me to the attention of the police and British soldiers and local Protestant militia namely the Ulster Defence Regiment (UDR.) In the early 1990s we campaigned against the militarisation of the border and the closing of our roads by the British army, forcing people to make long detours through checkpoints...

A number of us including human rights activists Oliver Kearney and Des Wilson formed a group calling itself EQUALITY to protest against the systematic discrimination against Catholics in employment. We organised in support of the MacBride Principles in the US. We organised a very effective Boycott of the Northern Bank in the six counties. (Boycott as a tactic that began in Ireland in 1870s when the people in county Mayo stopped paying rents to Captain Boycott). We were up against many forms of State violence including the state sponsored assassination of Catholics, politicians and lawyers, (including Pat Finucane and Rosemary Nelson) and civil rights workers.

During all this time we had to listen to a lot of baloney from Churchmen and politicians about crypto-provos and fellow travellers.

I had always believed that the only basis for lasting Peace in our situation was the withdrawal of the British from our country and the recognition by the Nations of the right of the people of Ireland as a whole to self-determination. Justice for me means an end to British rule in Ireland and the Irish people taking control and taking power in order to create an Ireland of Equals...It does not mean reform or crumbs from the master's table!

The Catholic Church preaches justice and issues encyclicals about justice -but it will never say what I am after saying. It will never apply it to the political situation because it will never upset the status quo. The Catholic Bishops have their own political agenda and their own reasons for accepting and even defending the status quo.

Resistance to British occupation has taken many different forms over the years. In Ireland men and women joined the IRA or some other armed group and took up arms to protect their own people and to resist the British occupation of Ireland. They have done so in every generation for centuries. Men and women have gone out and taken on the might of the British Empire. Many have given their lives. Many ended up in jail. Family life was disrupted.

The official church -the Bishops- denounced the men of violence meaning the IRA. Their denunciations of violence were one-sided. Some of us engaged in passive resistance. Passive resistance took the form of protests and a persistent demand for Equality. If the Irish Catholic Church had thrown its weight behind the demand for basic human rights and equality then there would have been no need for an armed resistance -or it would not have lasted so long but the official Catholic church in Ireland was compromised and was co-opted by the Brits even to opposing the Mac Bride Principles for Fair Employment.

Vatican II in the 1960s called on the church to act on behalf of the oppressed -but unlike in Latin America, the Irish bishops did not heed the call. It was in the aftermath of the Second Vatican Council that liberation theology emerged in some countries like Peru and Brazil in Latin America.

I have found that some of the ideas expressed in Liberation Theology bring a new dynamic into a situation of conflict. It is a real challenge to the dominant theology of church and State -the theology of obedience to authority...Liberation Theory takes away the fear of legalised authority.

Liberation Theory proclaims that the true God of the Bible is the God who takes sides —not any ethnic or national side but the God who takes the side of the poor and oppressed in their search for power. This was a real spiritual awakening for me...God spoke through those prophets who denounced the Oppressors of the poor. The Chosen people are the Oppressed People. The words of the prophet Amos take on a special meaning:

> *I hate and despise your feasts.*
> *I take no pleasure in your solemn festivals.*
> *When you offer me holocausts, I reject your oblations.*
> *Let me have no more of the din of your chanting,*
> *no more of your strumming on harps.*
> *But let Justice flow like water*
> *and INTEGRITY like an unfailing stream.*
> *Amos 5:21-24*

The preferential option for the poor is clearly seen in the life of Jesus of Nazareth which ended in his crucifixion as a subversive. Here was a man of integrity who faced the Political and Religious authorities of his day. He belonged to the Prophetic tradition in Judaism -the tradition that was prepared to speak out against the Oppressors of the people, those who crush the widow and the orphan.

Liberation Theology became a really powerful dynamic in places in Latin America where basic Christian communities were formed to reflect and act against injustice. We have the great example of Solentiname in Nicaragua and also of faith communities in Recife where Helder Camara was bishop and Sao Paulo, Brasil, where Cardinal Arns was bishop. In San Salvador small Christian groups met to listen to the word of God and to reflect. It was a way of building solidarity and increasing political awareness or conscientization.

Much of what I was doing in the 1970s and 1980s was linked with the work of Father

Des Wilson and the Springhill community in West Belfast where he lived. I was also involved in other Justice groups in Fermanagh and Tyrone and Derry. These were in a sense our basic Christian communities...where we exchanged views and organised several campaigns and took time out to reflect...and discuss the situation we were faced with and sometimes to discuss the meaning of our faith and the role of the churches. I cannot overstate how much I learned from the people about politics and about religion and about real solidarity. I learned more from them than I did at Maynooth College where I spent seven years preparing for my ministry as a priest!

I will mention three ways that Liberation Theology has inspired some of us in Ireland. Only a very small number of people took on the ideas of Liberation Theology in Ireland.

1. The first thing I found inspiring about Liberation Theology was its opposition to all forms of right-wing paternalistic theology which had grown up over the centuries and which justified the taking over of countries and the destruction of native cultures. In Ireland the Brits destroyed our language and our native legal system and our native system of land ownership. It was the same in other colonial enterprises when countries like Spain and Portugal set out to conquer and to civilise the world (Ref Things Fall Apart by Chinua Achebe also using the Bible to justify their rape and plunder!).

So Liberation Theology was about liberating theology from the stranglehold of the right wing Christian fundamentalists as well as liberating the oppressed from intolerable social conditions.

2. I discovered that Liberation Theology is based on a re-reading of the Bible from the point of view of the displaced and dispossessed and that this is the only true and authentic reading for the Word of God. Liberation theology is quite different to the kind of abstract theology we learned at school and in the Catholic seminary in Maynooth.

3. Thirdly, Liberation Theology offers us a context for dealing with armed resistance/struggle and makes clear distinctions between institutional/state violence and armed insurrection. I came to the conclusion that the decision to pursue armed resistance as an alternative to passive resistance in our situation was ultimately a question of conscience.

Conscience is the ultimate arbiter in these matters. Those who made this decision were not to be condemned for following their conscience to oppose tyranny. That has always been the teaching of the Catholic Church.

Those who are to be condemned are those who sit on the fence. They use all kinds of threats and abusive language. These are violent people who support the status quo. These are the moral cowards who would not lift a finger to rid their country of the tyranny. All they could do was collude with the tyranny because that is the net effect of their condemnations and vilification of the 'men of violence'.

Chauvinism/The Superior Race/The Chosen People

I am aware more than ever since I began preparing this talk that for the Palestinian people there is a problem with a particular form of Biblical theology and also with a Liberation Theology that has presented the Exodus story as a paradigm for liberation struggles. The narrow presentation of the Exodus as Gods chosen people achieving their freedom in a land of milk and honey raises very serious questions for all oppressed and dispossessed peoples and in particular for the Palestinian people who since 1967 have been dispossessed of their land and of their own state.

This has been carefully described and analysed in the late Fr. Michael Priors wonderful book *The Bible and Colonialism-A Moral Critique* (pub1997 by Sheffield Academic Press). After reading this book I realise how problematic some interpretations of the Bible are for Palestinian people and their struggle and for other people even ourselves in Ireland. Michael Prior refers to the Zionising of the Old Testament and the use of the Old Testament by the Colonisers and Missionaries down the centuries to the detriment of many indigenous and native peoples. The colonisers -along with the Christian missionaries used the Bible to justify their ruthless conquests in the name of spreading the gospel and civilisation.

National chauvinism -which can be seen in Old Testament story of Exodus and the conquest of the Promised Land—exists to this day and is now clearly seen in the attitude of the Christian Fundamentalists in the US and in the policies of the Bush regime in Iraq and elsewhere.

They create the notion that there is good and evil in the world and that they are good and those who oppose their vision of the new world order are the enemy who belong to the axis of evil. So in a way it does not matter if you are Irish republican or a Palestinian struggling to recover the land seized about 50 years ago or an Iraqi or Afghani wanting to end occupation of their countries, we all belong to the axis of evil. This is arrogance and chauvinism.

Our work in the pursuit of freedom is about empowerment and that is where Liberation Theology comes in.

Michael Prior calls us to set about re-reading of the Exodus in the light of the Palestinian experience -and indeed the colonial experience in many other places.

Michael Prior comments: However, the real poor of the Exodus narrative, surely, are the ones forgotten in the victory, The Canaanites and others, who are pushed aside or exterminated by the religious zeal of the invading Israelites with God on their side. The Bible itself is not value free and the Exodus narrative is disdainful of the rights of indigenous people. One should not be satisfied then with interpreting Black experience in the light of the Bible. Rather one must allow the Black experience to interrogate the Bible, and expose those traditions which are fundamentally oppressive.

Another writer who has dealt with this issue is Rosemary Radford Reuther whom I met over 30 years ago at our first ever LT conference in Ireland in 1976. After visiting the Middle East in 1988, Rosemary Reuther wrote (p104 C&Crisis April 14, 1988).

> For Palestinian Christians and Middle Easterners generally the issue raised by a Zionist use of Scripture is not the existence of God, which is taken for granted, but the nature of God. Is God a God of vengeance and war; a God who chooses one group of people at the expense of others; a Tribal God? Or is God a God of justice, truth and peace for all people, calling ALL people into relations of justice and peace with one another? The task of Biblical hermeneutics is to vindicate this second vision of God as the authentic one. It should provide the criteria for distinguishing this authentic vision from passages of the Bible which portray God as a tribal God who sides with the Jews against other peoples.

She goes on:

> For Palestinians Christians, the story of Biblical liberation sounds like a story of their own victimisation. Still worse, the God of Israel is said to be the author of this victimisation and injustice. God saves Israel by mandating the dispossession and slaughter of former inhabitants of the land

> The creation of the state of Israel and its history of take-over of Palestinian land and expulsion or repression of the Palestinian population has caused a crisis of belief for these near Eastern Christians. Many have responded to this contradiction by simply refusing to read the Old Testament in worship at all.

One Palestinian pastor and theologian who has tried to respond to this dilemma of biblical hermeneutics is Father Naem Ateek, rector of the Arab speaking congregation at St Georges Episcopal Cathedral in east Jerusalem.

There is a need for a dialogue within the global Christian community to call them to account for the way they have used Scripture to buttress Zionism and to ignore their Palestinian brothers and sisters.

The Possibilities of a Palestinian Liberation Theology

Albert Nolan reminds us that Liberation Theology is about reading the signs of the times -not just the bleak signs (like John the Baptist did) but the hopeful signs (like Jesus did). We should always look for signs of hope.

This conference is a sign of hope.

In Ireland we discovered that the way forward is through empowerment.

Justice, Equality and Freedom for all is the ultimate goal of any religion which appeals to the God of the Bible. The idea of any privileged nation or superior ethnic group is anathema to the Christian view of religion and the world. The idea of a superior nation who can devise a new World Order is anathema to the true Gospel of Jesus of Nazareth.

Another sign of hope? I have read in an article by Rosemary Radford Reuther about Fr Ateek's efforts to create and develop Palestinian liberation theology: Palestinian Christians need to reclaim for themselves the universalist God of Truth and Justice of the prophetic tradition and not identify the tribalistic God with Hebrew Scriptures as a whole. The God of the poor and the oppressed whose voice cries out through the prophet's texts against the powerful who expropriate the land of the poor and steal the sustenance of the widow and the orphan is of the greatest relevance to the Palestinians. Here they find God for themselves, concretely sharing their agony, demanding a justice for those who have been robbed and mistreated, demanding truth for those who have been the victims of lies and deceptions, demanding a new society of peace that can only be built on truth and justice.

How does such a Palestinian theology, like other Liberation Theologies on behalf of oppressed people, not become another tribalism, another claim that God is on our side against other communities of people, in this case on the side of the Palestinians against the Israelis? For Ateek and for all Liberation Theologians, the basic Christian supposition is that a tribal or nationalist concept of divine election is no longer theologically defensible. Divine partiality is contextual, not exclusive or related to one ethnic group. Rosemary Radford Reuther says this is an issue for Jews, Christians and Muslims. A Palestinian Christian Liberation Theology arising from an oppressed community seeking a just society in the midst of powerful aggressive states, Jewish and Muslim, may provide the key element in this needed dialogue...All three faiths will thereby be called to address their religious and nationalist exclusivism and to listen to the call of a God of Justice whose oneness transcends and overcomes all religious and ethnic division. (Rosemary R.Reuther C&C April 4 1988.)

Conclusion

My good friend, Des Wilson, who has been a priest in Belfast for over 50 years always says: You know Joe, We are too nice. We are too nice to our oppressors...You get nowhere by being nice - and you know he is right. His great quote is the Truth will set you free and Des believes in telling it like it is...Telling the truth and accepting the consequence. That is the way to freedom.

It is amazing what a small number of people dedicated to the truth and to an alternative vision can achieve -in raising consciousness, in giving courage and in neutralising the impact of those Church leaders and political leaders and commentators who support the status quo, that is what I have learned and that is the message I want to share with you my brothers and sisters.

I want to share this quote I found recently with you:

The Cherokee word for land also means history, culture and religion. We have no history, no culture if we have no land for them to come from. We cannot think of ourselves as existing without existing directly in the land. Land for us is not just property or even a place to build a house or plant crops. It is something truly sacred in the profound sense, and it is a part of ourselves.

Jimmie Durham, IFDA Dossier 6 April 1979, quoted in Food, Poverty and Power (1982)

***

Let me say with regard to the Irish Liberation struggle, that we do not yet have peace in Ireland. We have a peace process which I broadly support —but we do not have peace or an end to British occupation. The peace process came about after many years of struggle and sacrifice by Irish republicans -and after years of internal debate and discussion within Irish republicanism especially among Irish republican prisoners. This discussion which became more intense after the 1981 Hunger-strike was about tactics and strategy. With the increasing military activity of the IRA in Britain, the Brits had shown a willingness to negotiate after years of saying they would never talk to terrorists.

The internal debate and political moves by Gerry Adams and Sinn Fein led to the first important Ceasefire in many years on 1 Sept 1994. This broke down in 1996 when the Brits showed bad faith. It was restored in 1998 when Blair became PM and was followed soon after by the Belfast /Good Friday Agreement.

The Agreement provided for power -sharing in the 6 counties and North-South bodies. It provided for a Bill of Rights and a new policing service in the six counties (which still has not come into being).

All of this was risky for republicans. They risked a serious split in their ranks. But Sinn Fein and the IRA had weighed up the pros and cons and decided that to achieve the ultimate goal of Irish freedom and reunification they would have to become a political force and win over the Irish people to the idea and get the support of Irish-America. The leadership was able to bring most of their members with them in pursuit of this strategy.

In this way they would confront the British about their role in Ireland and demand their withdrawal. Sinn Fein has been calling on the Dublin government to provide a Paper on Irish Unity and how best that unity can be achieved. Up till now the Dublin political establishment has baulked at the idea. They have always been good at rhetoric and could get away with the rhetoric about wanting to see a unified Ireland but they have never spelled out how they intend bringing this about.

Since the Unionists led by David Trimble collapsed the institutions set up under the Good Friday Agreement in 2003, the main focus of the governments in London and Dublin, as well as the Media, has been on the IRA and Sinn Fein. Sinn Fein's vote has risen dramatically and this has sent shock –waves throughout the Irish political establishment -especially the Fianna Fail party and the Progressive Democrats which form the coalition government. There has been a constant attack on Sinn Fein in recent months.

Paisleys right wing DUP has become the largest pro-Union party in the 6 counties and so far has refused to share power or work the Belfast Agreement. The hope is that they will respect the mandate of Irish republicans and nationalists and implement the Belfast Agreement.

The British had to enter negotiations with Irish republicans. They said they would never talk to them. The Israelis along with their allies in the US and Britain are going to have to negotiate with the Palestinian people and their representatives. The question is when. In order to avoid further bloodshed and loss of life and suffering it should be sooner rather than later.

Presentation

Dr Ilan Pappe

Former Political Science senior lecturer at Haifa University. Currently Professor of History at University of Exeter, UK.

Abstract

- Dr Pappe argues that the education system is an important and useful tool in the defeating the ideological foundations of Zionism and the ensuing Islamophobia that informs Israeli culture. (Pg 4).
- Dr Pappe calls for 'imposing of sanctions on Israel like those who were imposed on South Africa' (sic Pg 2). He further argues that 'the UN and Britain have particular responsibility for forcing Israel.... to allow the Palestinian refugees to return.
  Dr Pappe extends an effective role and responsibility to states and collective international state structures.

I am very happy to be here and I want to thank the organisers for inviting me, I apologise for... mainly to the other speakers and the participants in this conference that I won't be here all this morning. This has to do with my impossible attempt to be both in Cairo and in London on the same day and I fly this afternoon to Cairo to a UN conference on peace where I deliver more or less the same speech that I will deliver here but given that this is a UN conference with Israelis and Palestinians and Egyptians in Cairo I was not allowed and I couldn't give a speech entitled 'the hidden layers of Israeli phobia from the right to return'. UN agenda on peace today does not recognise, unfortunately the Palestinian right of return and therefore I had to use an innocent title such as 'Is there a shift in the UN peace efforts'. This is more or less what I am going to talk about today. And I think the fact that it is taking place in Cairo under the auspices of the UN with Palestinian and Israeli delegates tells the whole story of the right of return in many ways.

I am talking about hidden layers and not obvious layers of Israeli attitudes towards the right of return not because I underrate the obvious layers or the layers that are open to us as a book. They are important, they are significant but I think within this community of listeners they are perfectly known to you, I will mention them to you in few words. What is obvious in Israeli objection to the right of return. But I think the, what I call the hidden layers tell a far more important story not just the story about the Israeli attitudes towards the Palestinians throughout the last 57 years but rather the story of Israel and Zionism within the Arab World, within the middle east and within the Muslim world. And I think the right of return, or rather the Israeli attitude towards the right of return holds the key to understanding Zionism in Israel vis a vis not only the Palestinian world, and not only the Arab world but the Muslim world as a whole.

The obvious layers of the Israeli objection to the right of return have to do with the need to continue as a state and as a society, the denial of what Israel had done in 1948. This is quite obvious that society and its leadership does not want to face a chapter of ethnic cleansing especially by a community that succeeded in winning the title or the status of the ultimate victim of the 20th century due to the Holocaust in Europe. And therefore the right of return, in the eyes of the Israelis is not just a permission for the Palestinians to return to home, to villages and towns all through the homeland of Palestine it is, more importantly an admission by Israel of the massive expulsions of Palestinians in 1948, of the destruction of 531 villages, 20 urban neighbourhoods, and 11 towns, and the displacements of almost _ of a million people, and actually its much more than that as after 1948 the ethnic cleansing continued and expulsion continued into the mid 1950's and in fact it never stopped because in 1957 there was a renewed ethnic cleaning and I'm sure this distinguished crown does not need me to tell them how exactly this awful chapter continued.

The strategies for challenging the obvious layers of Israeli rejection of the right of return are also quite clear. I, myself am involved in an educational effort in Israel to try and push forward the acknowledgement among the Israeli, Jewish society about what happened in 1948. On a more political level I am part or many others, I think, outside the Middle East and inside the Middle East trying to push forward the concept of accountability of the Israelis namely that they should not only acknowledge the fact that they have expelled the Palestinians but should allow repopulation of the refugees as the best form of showing, of taking the responsibility for what they have done in 1948. It's probably needless to say, but I will say it that none of this is possible before the Israeli military occupation of the West Bank and the Gaza Strip will end. And as I stated before and I never miss an opportunity to say it wherever I see more than two people sitting in front of me, the only way of ending the Israeli military occupation is by turning Israel into a pariah state by imposing on it sanctions like those who were imposed on South Africa during the heydays of Apartheid because anything else will fail. I say this also about the military struggle to liberate the occupied territories; I don't think it has a chance. And also the diplomatic efforts to convince the Israelis to withdraw from the occupied territories. Those two ways are futile and every passing day is one day too many in the history of the occupation. Now, why do I insist that this is not enough, as an activist, as a Jewish activist in Israel I think what is said right now is the full agenda, and if I will be witnessing in my own life time even 1% of what I put forward maybe the end of military occupation, the Palestinian return to their homeland I should be satisfied personally, but I fear that this is not enough. That this is not enough and this is why I talk about hidden layers of the Israeli and Jewish attitude towards the right of return.

I think this is connected to the whole notion of creating a Jewish state among the Arab states in the late 19th century. Long before the Palestinians where expelled in 1948 the problem of the Palestinian right of return, so to speak was created at the very fact that the group of Jewish activists in late 19th century Europe decide that they will build a European state in the midst of the Arab world at the expense of the

Palestinians. It was very easy to sell this idea in the late 19th century because it was during the time of colonialism, and the idea of implementing European political structure in the midst of the Arab world was not alien to the policies of the colonial empires at the time, Britain and France. But as the decolonialisation process in the Middle East progressed and as the anti liberation movements in the Middle East succeeded in expelling most of their British and French occupiers, it was a very wise and manipulative policy by the Jewish community in Palestine to secure the assistance of US and other European powers in order to maintain such a European structure in the midst of the Arab world despite the decolonialisation and by the time the last European soldier left the middle east in 1971 the Jewish state had already been not effectively been completed but already possessed the strongest military army in the area, and had concluded a strategic alliance with the US that enabled it to sustain any attempt to dismantle it or to force it to withdraw from areas it had occupied in Palestine and from other Arab countries.

Therefore the right of return is connected to this idea that you can have a Jewish Western enclave, Judaism as we've heard in this respect is defined as an ethnicity or as national group rather than as a religion, so Judaism as an ethnicity or as nationalism, needed a structure of a state in order to be able to do two things, to take over Palestine and disposes the Palestinians and for that you needed a state, not only an army, not only an American assistance, and secondly in order to have a state, it needed a shape according to its founders that extended even beyond Palestine itself. Now, that was one problem or one strategy that the Jewish state succeeded in maintaining more or less, with some problems but, basically with a very successful history, ever since the creation of the state since 1948, or one can even say ever since the creation of the Jewish community as a separate political entity in Palestine at the very beginning of the 20th century. But in order to sustain this idea of a European or a Western Jewish political entity in the midst of the Arab world at the expense of the Palestinian and with a very tense relationship with the Arab world around it, in order to sustain it you didn't only need to occupy territory, you didn't only need to dispossess people and colonise them, you needed also to secure ethnic supremacy, and ethnic exclusivity and for that reason the Jewish state developed a set of laws and pursued a number of policies that were meant to maintain what the Israelis called a solid Jewish majority in Palestine because of the wish to be part of the European and Western World the Israelis were careful never to talk about a pure Jewish state, namely a state that does not to have any Palestinians in it, although inside Israel the discourse is very clear about the need to have a country that is totally Jewish and where dispossession of the Palestinians is complete, it is very clear to everyone that in order to achieve the goal of being part of the West, or part of the so called civilised world and so on there is a limit to how you can pursue ethnic cleansing when they are exercised not in times of war but in times of relative peace and even in times of war there is a limit to ethnic cleansing as the Jews released in 1948.

So the problem is, and this is a serious problem, in fact I think it occupies now the strategic agenda of the Israeli policy makers, I mean there's a tactical agenda which has to do with who would form which government and so on, and I'm talking about the strategic agenda which involves the academia, the literati, the political establishments, and this is how best placed questions of peace efforts, of occupation of refusal to give up Palestine territory on one hand and the wish to maintain, what I called before a solid Jewish majority on the other, as I've said full scale ethnic cleansing is out of the question at least in the near future as long as Israel continues to be the way it is now but there are, there are situations where even the wish to be, to maintain the image of the civilised state, or as a member of the Western community of states or a member of the community of so called civilised states, there are moments where even this wish would be put aside if the sense would be in Israel, that there is a danger of losing the ethnic vast majority or any processes that can undermine the state ideology and state judiciary system that supports the supremacy, policies and ideology of Zionism in other worlds Israel doesn't have a constitution but it has constitutional laws and non-constitutional laws and practises which make sure that within a certain demographic balance mainly where the Palestinians are more of less 15 to 20 percent of the population their significant numbers do not affect the Jewish supremacy in the land. Let's give you one example, this is a constitutional law that says the land of Israel belongs to the Jewish people and not to the state of Israel hence this cannot be sold or transacted with Arabs in Israel, so the fact that there are 20% so called Israeli Arab citizens that does not allow the same rights to land acquisition, ownership and possession as it allows to the Jewish citizens of Israel.

Now, immigration is a very important fact in this game now, therefore it took a very long and extensive effort to convince even Israelis that the illogical equation by which Israeli absorbed 1 million immigrants from Russia and yet refuses to allow the return of 1 million Palestinians, this would be seen as an illogical equation. It was an illogical equation even according to the Zionist discourse because so many of those people who came into the land of Israel were not Jews, we know that, we see many of them in the churches, those Jews who came from the ex-Soviet Union. And the reason they were brought was not because they were Jews, and this tells you something about the definition of Judaism as ethnicity and nationalism, which unfortunately I won't have time to elaborate, the reason that they were brought was that they were not Arabs, this is was important in a supremacy ethnic state, the important thing is not who you are but who you are not, an ethnic state or an ethnic dictatorship is founded in order to maintain a ethnic majority and out of fear of another ethnic group and that as long as the people that come in do not belong to that ethnic group which it dispossessed, occupied and colonised they are legitimate citizens of your own state, therefore there are so many "Jews" in Israel who are not Jews they are people who came from Thailand, Philippines, they are Christians who came from Russia and Latvia, there are Christians of whom some of them came from Ethiopia, there are so many secular Jews for whom Judiasim has nothing to do with religion, but one thing is very clear about all these people, they are not Arab, but they're problems of course. In 1950's, well, because of the Holocaust and because of Israel's failure to bring enough Jews from Europe, decided to bring 1 million Jews from Arab countries, now these Jews are of course Arab, from an ethnic point of view these Jews were Arab, this is what the Israeli discourse is all about so there was a very concentrated effort to de-Arabise these Jews, you had to de-Arabise otherwise you'd lose the solid ethnic majority and unfortunately the processes by which the Jews from the Arab countries were de-

Arabised were so successful, this is why we find so many Arab Jews at the forefront of politics, of anti-Arab politics, and anti-Palestinian politics in Israel because it was very clear that the ticket into fooling them into the Jewish society in Israel was to show a very clear animosity, hatred and opposition to the Palestinian and Arab world and positions so therefore we have this problem.

Now let me end by saying how do we challenge such a formidable task by which we can see that the Israeli the Palestinian refugees can return, not because they have a different perception of peace, not only because they fear to admit the crimes that they've commit in 1948 but mainly because they don't want to be part of Middle East, part of the Arab world into which they settled by force, uninvited. How do we deal with such a problem, I can only give you my personal perspective from within, of course there are other perspectives and some of them I'm sure you will hear today. How do I deal with it as an Israeli Jew who was born in Israel a few years ago?

One I think is to deal with questions which the architects of the peace process in the Middle East tell us are not relevant for peace making. We should tell them that these questions are very relevant such is the question of what political structure for the question of Palestine. I deal with it by saying that my idea of a one state solution is not a Utopia it is not something that should be dealt with in the far distant future, it is something that should be dealt with tomorrow morning because it is within a one state structure and there is variance of a one state structure which I would not go into, within one state structure there is a possibility of defeating the ethnic supremacy and ideology of Israel.

Secondly, I do wish as a member of that community to absorb the fears of Jews in Israel we heard that many of these fears, and I agree, are fears that were put or planted in the hearts of people by a very fierce and manipulative system of indoctrination, no doubt about it, but nevertheless these are fears, even if an evil system has produced phobic people the phobia is real even if the system itself was manipulative and had very sinister reasons for planting these fears inside people. Now dealing with fears of people is not easy and anyone who has visited Israeli and knows members of the 7 million Jews who live there know how deeply rooted are these fears of anything Arab, of anything Muslim, and I dedicate my life also within the educational system to trying to defeat this system of indoctrination by finding ways of challenging Islamaphobia and Arabphobia in Israel but again unfortunately I don't have the time to tell you how I do this.

The third one is, we have to challenge these activists inside and outside the hegemonic discourse of the peace making. I've already talked about the one state solution as something that is totally sidelined and marginalised from the discourse of peace in the Middle East. The second issue is of course the right of return, the UN and Britain have been particularly responsible for forcing Israel to allow at least in principle but definitely also afterwards in practice the right of the Palestinians refugees people to return, that's relocation at the centre of the agenda now if our politicians don't do that we at the NGO can do that. And if the media doesn't do it there is a whole world of internet and other ways of putting this forward as the main issue.

There is the question of representation of villages and some of them we've heard today and I think one thing I will take with me back to Palestine and Israel although I missed most of the lectures of the distinguished keynote speaker and I apologise for this I think the whole idea of the chosen people being the oppressed people is a beautiful notion and I will take that with me because I find activists in Palestine that this notion of the oppressed people being the chosen people allows me, members of Islamic movement in Israel, members of the left within the Palestinian communities, secular Jews, all kinds of other people, it allows us to form a coalition to fight against the occupation, against the racist and supremacy policies of the state of Israel despite the differences of opinion, despite the differences of future scenarios and future visions of how exactly we would like to be part of the Middle East but it allows us to locate, to trace evil where it exists and fight with all our hearts and all our means against that evil regardless of the fact of whether we are Muslims, Christians or Jews and this is why the Palestinian refugees, for me as an Israeli Jew, are the chosen people, and I think it also means that if we deal as a coalition we are dealing with future questions of the Middle East as a whole. The Middle East has many Muslim people, it has Christian minorities, it has Jewish majorities, it has religious people, it has non-religious people. It's high time that everyone that lives in the Middle East including the Jews who live in Palestine partake in the problem of how to build a better Middle East for all of us instead of going to Eurovision, playing football in Europe and dreaming of an earthquake that would take them away from the Middle East and attach them to god knows where, Russia or Italy.

Now I will end with the occupation, this very long road to redemption for all of us, and we all need redemption whether we are very religious people or not very religious people. We need divine help given the formidable tasks in front of us as people of the Middle East and as people of the Middle East only we as the people of the Middle East will solve the problem of the area nobody else's F 16s and tanks will solve for us our problems, decide for us our political structure and tell us what is our moral vision and future and we will decide by ourselves. But in order to begin this very long road to redemption we first have to end the Israeli military occupation, everyone who has been there knows that every day it brings with it new crimes against humanity that has to be stopped and every one, you have to be an ambassador, an ambassadress in a relentless struggle to stop this occupation before we talk about peace, reconciliation and even the right of return. We should not let off any representative of Israel, anyone who is talking in the name of a Israel to feel that he is welcome anywhere until the military occupation ends with no conditions attached.

PART TWO:

The Right to Return, Universality and Liberation

Rabbis Weiss and Cohen from the group Neturei Karta, develop a Jewish theological perspective on Zionism and the Right to Return with an emphasis on spiritual and doctrinal matters. Rabbi Weiss and Rabbi Cohen understand the character of Zionism to be unjust and misguided but simultaneously emphasis that Zionism is a direct challenge to providence and the divine decree of exile as well as a stain on Judaism.

In highlighting the failure to implement UN resolutions regarding the right to Palestinian refugees to return, the May El-Khansa implicitly assumes and accepts role of the international community but, unlike Pappe highlights it as ineffective. Her understanding of Zoinism as with McVeigh, Cassiem and Ameli posits it in the role of neo-colonialist discourse.

Judaism, Zionism and The Right of Return

Rabbi Yisroel Weiss

Neturei Karta, USA

Abstract

- Palestinian tragedy places a stain not only on Judaism but on the very concept of Holiness.
- Palestinians right to return is an issue of religion.
- UN rejects the significance of religion and the role of the Torah as articulated by Rabbi's.
- UN seek to deal with 'human rights' issues in the context of prevailing realities and practicalities.
- However, religion has been used a basis for justifying the creation and continued existence of the state of Israel.
- Moreover, Zionists have actively used religion as a rallying point to build a nation and nationalism.
- Religion has been used covertly used by the Zionist state to inculcate fear.

With God's help, I pray to God that he bestows upon me his wisdom and allows me to convey this to this August gathering and that his word, his truth should go out to the world and to sanctify his name with this. Amen. Asalaam Allaikum.

They have asked me to speak about the right of return of the Palestinian people. First I want to thank Massoud, Islamic Human Rights Committee and all the others who are involved here and the organizations for honouring me and giving me this privilege to be able to speak here and for all you I thank who have come to listen. It's for us a great honour because we know that with our words, by revealing the truth that is breaking this myth that is prevalent throughout the world we are sanctifying God's name, so I thank you all.

The fact of the matter is that the issue called The Right of Return speaks about a problem, a very unfortunately a great tragedy for the Palestinian people, a great tragedy really for the Jewish people. For us it is a double tragedy because what is being done to the Palestinian people is not only, that human beings that are suffering, it is being done in our name and the name of the Jewish people, in the name of Judaism. This is a stain on Judaism, it's a stain on holiness and we are obligated by God to try and let, to correct this first misnomer to clarify the truth that this is nothing to do with Godliness, to correct the truth and to try with God's help, as God requires of us to always try to accomplish. But we must do what we could to correct the situation.

The word, Right of Return, which is being taken away from the Palestinian people, speaks about the issue about a religion really. Although people, some people around the world are going to argue that this does not, this has nothing to do with religion. It's human rights and, it's people, the Israeli people who are living in the lands now and therefore the question of religion is really not to be brought up and there are people that say everything has to do with religion and then raises the question of religion. But many times in the United Nations or other places people say they don't want to hear it's not relevant about what the Torah has to say, what God, the Godliness is involved here has nothing to do with this because of its practicality. It's people that are living in the land, and people who are not living there now, we just have just look what's practical. But the truth if you will, just listen to the words that are being spoken about the Right of Return, they will understand that insidiously the Zionist community is bringing in the issue of religion. But they just don't want to bring it to the forefront, they only use it whenever they have to, to put fear into people, so that the people are afraid to stop with the stop, the fight with God and therefore they don't have to usually speak about it openly.

Many times when we went to the United Nations, although there it's purely human rights issues, they don't want to speak about religion. But at the end of the day when somebody starts saying that it's pure racism not to let the Palestinian people return and how come, how can you take away the right of the people to return to their land. There are always say what do you mean, the Jewish people were there before it was Godly given to them a few thousand years ago.

So therefore we would just like to first of all clarify on the point of religion. On the issue of why they say that the Jewish people throughout the world were not born in the land of Palestine, really doesn't matter, they always, they always have the right of return. While the Palestinian and the Arab people don't have the right of return. Even if they lived here, and it was their houses and they have the keys to their houses. So let's just clarify first of all the religious issue here. The time is very short and I blame the Zionists again for that. They don't let us talk when there are so many issues to speak about, of course we can't, but we will try with God's help to bring up a little about this issue. And all of you I'm very sure, according to the Torah, according to the Jewish belief and we are talking here about Judaism which real Judaism is a belief. It's not a nationality, it's something which was known throughout the generations as not a nationality, not a materialistic issue, it was a belief and in this belief God gave the Jewish people, made a bond with the Jewish people, commanded us to be a kingdom of priests as a whole nation and when God gave us this commandment, every human being is to inherit the world, to come with the righteous, we believe that every person has to serve God. But we accepted an extra yoke, an extra bond of six hundred and thirty commandments of the Torah where we must be a nation of priests and when God made this bond with us, and he said that I am giving you my land, my garden, where God's spirit rests. God's spirit is all over the world but specially rests in the land of Palestine and the land of Israel and he said send out the people, I am sending out the people who have [done wrong] to you because they have defiled the land. And in order for you to be able to stay in this land you must be on a high elevation of pureness of holiness, and if not then you will be expelled from the land. This repeated many times, it says this in the Bible; anybody can open the Bible, the Old Testament and see this. And this was God's stipulation with the Jewish people. Eventually as the Jewish people accepted this stipulation, accepted this bond with God to watch the commandments and eventually there was the prophets as again you can read the prophets, Ezekiel, Jeremiah, all the prophets, they all spoke about their how God would warn them through the prophets that they, they are not up to the level of holiness that is required and they will be expelled, eventually they were expelled and when God expelled the Jewish people from the land of Israel he specifically, put on them on the oath that they are forbidden to return on mass to the land, as individuals they can return, but not on mass, they are forbidden to go against any nation or make any attempt to [deny] existence [of] the decree of God.

The Jews accepted this for two thousand years and then a movement called Zionism started by people who were non-religious, people who ignored the Torah who not only left the walls of Judaism but, they detested Judaism. You can see this in their writing. They decided that they wanted to [say] that they are sick and tired of Jewish suffering, instead of hoping that any suffering that happens to human beings is from God and it's just to remind us to repent. They, they, they excluded God from this equation, they excluded God from anything that happens on this world, everything is material by them and therefore they said the reason we have to leave Israel two thousand years ago was because we were physically weak; which is blasphemous. We know that it's clear, anyone who is God fearing can study the books of the prophets knows we were sent out because of our sins. It has nothing to do with physical inaptness. But they of course as I say were heretics and they decided that the problem was a materialistic problem of physical weakness; the solution obviously, is to be physical strong. And therefore, they make a strong army, a strong nation. Now let's understand this was not really the whole issue here, the Zionists who decided to create the state of Israel, the Zionists, they are called Zionists because of Zion returning to the land of Palestine, Zion, Jerusalem, is referred as such in the Torah, Jerusalem is Zion. These people, they really were just interested in having a piece of land. Their role was to take this Jewish Nation of God fearing people and to transform, and then uproot the religious message, transform the concept the Judaism as a religion into a nationality, something which is devoid of godliness. This was their goal, their ultimate goal and to reach this goal they lived here, mow down Jews, mow down the Arabs, anything. This was their ultimate goal.

Of course one of the issues, as I say, they have to have a safe haven. So that they decided that they will go to Uganda, of course, because that is practical. But they realized that the Jewish people won't follow them if they go to a land in Africa. What are the people going to follow them for? Some people may follow them, but they won't get the Jewish nation to follow them. The Jewish people though who are expelled, who are true to God, we know that we were expelled from the land of the Israel but eventually we believe and we yearn and we hope not to return to have a stake, have a piece of land to have a property. This is not our goal. Our goal as a Jewish people is to serve God and the ultimate service of God is when God's name will be glorified throughout the world and the whole world will recognize one God. And this will happen we believe, ultimately, God will make a metaphysical change in the world where the entire world, all of a sudden will wake up one day and recognize the one God and serve in the harmony. And then all people will go out, according to the Jewish belief to Palestine and serve him in harmony. This is our goal that we pray for, we do not, and we are forbidden to make any attempts to bring this about, only through prayer. So we yearn and pray for this. This is what we strive for, but we do have to take any action and obviously we don't take any action to have a piece real estate; to have a materialistic piece of land. So the whole concept of just taking land away is just strange to the Jewish beliefs. But the Zionists when they decided that they wanted to make this religion into a nationality and realized that God will not serve their purpose, because the nation, the Jewish nation won't follow them. They decided it's very, very smart and practicable, they counted on the ignorance that people will not look further to see what it says in the books that it was taken from us and that we are forbidden to go and take this back and whoever is living there, the indigenous people, they are rightful owners of this land, without a question. It's their land totally. God has given them right to be there. Eventually all humanity will return but that's a whole different story.

That will happen without me having to convince anybody, it will happen when there is a metaphysical change in the world. So one ultimate point in the Torah is very clear, the land is forbidden to us, it's a forbidden fruit, and it's forbidden for us to attempt to take it. So what does that mean? That means the right of return. And what they say that the Jews have the right of return and not the Palestinians is a farce. It belongs to the people of Palestine; it belongs to the indigenous people, the Arab people. So therefore when you come to the United Nations and you have human rights activists who are afraid to talk about this right of return, you have human activists because they are afraid the work for Rwanda, the work for Darfur, which are very important, but when it comes to Palestine people are a little afraid because they are afraid that maybe they're taking away from the Jewish people what's theirs. They don't want to start up with God. We want to inform you that not only are we not starting up with God; you are doing God's work when you are standing up to the right of return for the Palestinians. Let me inform you that really, the Slugnasood was not sure that it should be an Islamic right of return, let it ride as it was Islamic human rights, this human right, it's not human rights, it's Godly rights. It belongs to the Palestinian people because this is what God who created the world says and we as Jewish people, we would be forbidden to have this land even if it would have been a desolate land, unsettled land because we are forbidden to have even the smallest entity of our kingdom because we are under a decree of exile. And again we are never waiting for the old state of Israel in the future either. And it happens to be they have compounded this terrible prize, this terrible tragedy, because it happened to be that this land was a settled land, there were the Palestinian people, there were Arab people living together with Jewish people there. Yeah.

There were Jewish people living, I should say amongst the Arab people, the vast majority, of course was the Muslim people living there and we know the Jewish community knew all along and we never strayed from the teachings of the Torah we know what was rightfully theirs, we are forbidden to steal from the Palestinian people, so it was a double tragedy, unfortunately, our wayward brethren are straying from the Torah and going away, even if it would have been desolate and certainly in this case, where it was settled and they are committing one crime upon the other, when they are oppressing these people, expelling, subjugating them, this is all, all contrary to the picture of the Jew who must as a nation of priests, who…are supposed to emulate God and emulating God to be compassionate.

Every aspect of the Torah is being broken by the Zionists. We want you to know that. We want you, I, there is no time left, the first Rabbi on our site www.nkusa.org, you have a lot of documents, you have the first, important, main documents we can say that was in the UN in 1947 before the imminent creation of the state. I spoke to Rabbis who were there at the time. I had the privilege of speaking with our senior Rabbi who was a student of Rabbi Deschinski, he was there when the Untied Nations sent the delegation to Palestine to ask the community what they wanted. He was there on the right, he should have many healthy long years and he said I stood this with Rabbi Deschski and we sent a letter to the United Nations, document, A-AC-14-44, to the Secretary General, of The Untied Nations, "we" write the Jewish Orthodox Community of Jerusalem comprising sixty thousand souls object to the decree of including Judaism as a Jewish state, they didn't call it a state, they called a Jewish state and it's becoming residents automatically citizens of the Jewish state. Our community demands that Judaism being a national zone under your protection. When they saw that they had no word of the United Nations that they were going to create this state. They said I am the chief rabbi Jerusalem give us a free Jerusalem. We worked as relatively free citizens in the national zone of Jerusalem. We worked to live amongst the Arabs which is the godly right, the godly wish. This is what real Orthodox Jews and finder Rabbi Deschski, Chief Rabbi Deschski, in the name of the community. This, and the fight continues, we have pictures that just occurred, our Jews are beaten till today, they are been beaten bloody, bludgeoned and people are killed. This is all the name of Zionists against the religious community. There are hundreds and thousands of people who are still standing true to this, unfortunately, there are some religious, many religious people who not because they are Zionists, in fact they don't sent their children to the army, they don't join the government because they have to have representation because they were being strangled by the existing government just as Palestinian people have representation. Unfortunately, and these are the ones that you find in the government, they say don't return land to the Arabs, why, there is no time to get into this but I just want to touch upon this. Many of these people they have the fear factor, they are being told that Muslims want to kill the Jews, that Muslims constantly say the Jews, the Jews; they want to kill every Jew. So even though they are not Zionists and they will celebrate with us the dismantlement of state, but they are afraid to return not, not that they don't support the state but they are afraid because they have been influenced by the propaganda of the Zionists. So therefore I want you to know that it is very important for few reasons to understand, that to clarify. The problem here is not the religion Judaism and its many hundreds of thousands of Jewish people that still stand true with you, we feel your suffering, and it hurts us, every bit of blood, every Palestinian child and every person that is suffering there.

We have a rabbi over here that was himself imprisoned and beaten there who shares with you. But it's important for you to know this difference and clarify when you speak that it's the difference, it's not a religious difference. Even though we mention before our differences, we have a total different interpretation of the Torah but it's not a religious conflict we have been living for hundreds of years and thousands of years together. It's not a religious conflict, it's just what the Zionists are trying to ensnare the world and make it look like a religious argument that can't be solved. Let the world know it's not a religious argument, if there were never any human rights activists and nobody to stand up; we would all be living together in peace. Since Zionism the inception of this political movement, this transformation of religion into a political movement, godless entity, this is the cause of suffering. Be clear in the words, it will help you as Muslim people to be recognised in the world as civilised people which the Zionists are trying to misconstrue. And we know the truth that you are civilised, you have been our save haven, now close friends with the Jewish people and we are appreciative for hundreds of years. Where have we found safe haven amongst the Muslim's nations are, we are all amongst Muslim community and the Jewish community we know this, we are thankful for this. So be careful and always speak so that they can't accuse you... of being. Say we know the truth, say don't accuse us... Don't ask what it says in the Koran about Judaism and so forth because this existed before, before it was Zionism we were living in peace. Let's solve the issues, the rights the godly rights of the Palestinian people have been taken from them, nothing to do with religion, nothing to do with a religious conflict; they have nothing to do with this. The rights, these people were living in a land, it was their land and it should be returned to them, don't try to confuse the subject with religion.

...We should again be able to live together in peace. And as I say the Muslim people themselves who are suffering the wrong betrayal of them, it will corrected if we clarify that it is nothing to do with the Muslims being vicious people like the Zionists are saying, on the contrary. They are just begging for what's right.

We pray and you should all pray together with us because ultimately as I say accomplishment is only by God. We pray to the speedy and peaceful dismantlement of this state of Israel, this illegitimate state, the transformation back to the self rule of the proper owners of the land. Which God could make it happen. We only know that anything that is against God cannot have a long existence. When it will happen, how it will happen, I don't know. Let's pray that it should... with the suffering should stop..., let us pray... Let us pray for the day when God's glory should be revealed throughout the world and all humanity will recognise the one God and that should happen speedily in our time and we should all be successful in our endeavours to sanctify God, Amen. Thank you.

The Common Denominator: Humanitarian Approaches to Palestine from Jewish and other Faith Traditions

Rabbi Cohen

Neturei Karta, UK

Abstract

The Jewish faith forbids Zionism on the basis of both doctrinal beliefs and religious/ethical values. The aim of Zionism is to impose "secular but sectarian" rule over the indigenous Palestinian population and is contrary to Jewish beliefs.
A basic part of Jewish belief is that the present state of exile is a "heavenly decree" which should be willingly accepted with humility.

The Jewish concept of the nation is that of a religious group bonded by faith. Religion is the establishing force behind the Jewish national identity. The existence of a territorially organised nation is irrelevant to the Jewish concept of the nation.

For 2000 years the Jewish people have been without land but have been able to retain their distinct identity based on religion. In retaining their religion the Jewish nation has retained its (national) identity.

Zionism attempts to create a new secular Jewish identity based not on religion but on land. Zionism abandons the orthodox approach to exile. (In as much as it deviate from divine providence to take the law into its own hand, the Zionist project can be understood a posing a threat to orthodox Jewish beliefs and the Jewish identity.)

Humanitarianism is a common denominator in all religious traditions. In order to conceive an "ill conceived nationalistic ambition, a shocking contravention of Jewish religious values was committed by the Zionists".

In agreement with the Neturei Karta position most orthodox Jews do not in principle agree with to the existence of a Zionist state. However a range of opinions exist how to deal with the reality of the Zionist state of Israel. Opinions range from "positive to operation, to pragmatic acceptance, to total opposition in every way". According to the Torah and the Jewish faith the present Palestinian/Arab claim to rule Palestine is right and just. The Zionist claim is wrong and criminal. Neturei Karta attitude to Israel is that it is a flawed and illegitimate concept.

The noble attendees of I think this outstanding conference on the theological approach to the confrontation that exists in Palestine, between Zionists and the Palestinian people. It's my honour and privilege to have the opportunity of addressing you on this subject and I of course thank our friend Massoud and I'm very grateful to him for giving me the opportunity of addressing you this afternoon.

Some of the things I'm going to say may duplicate to some degree what my colleague Rabbi Weiss has mentioned but perhaps with a slightly different stress with a slightly different approach and repetition does not necessarily mean harm. Its particularly relevant for me to be able to talk about the theological approach to this matter, to the matter of the confrontation in Palestine, because the very reason why I and my colleagues at the Neturei Karta try to make every effort to take part in discussions such as this is because that we feel we have a religious and religion based humanitarian duty to publicise our message as much as possible and by doing so to remove the stain which we feel blots the image of the Jewish people.

Our very raison d'etre is to bring out the practical application of our theological approach. So firstly I hope we pray that with the creator's help my words and our discussions here today can be correct and true in their content and in their conclusion. Another reason why the opportunity to talk today is important is because the theological approach does not always coincide with the political attitudes and for us it is the theological reality and truth, as we consider it, that is all important. Firstly my friends the short and simple theological message from orthodox Jewry is that Zionism and Judaism are total opposites incompatible and diametrically opposed. Zionism is not Judaism in any way and as a corroboratory to this statement though not strictly relevant to today's discussion anti-Zionism is not anti-Semitism.

You may note that we do not talk about orthodox Judaism which could imply a certain brand of a Judaism as opposed to other brands; we talk about orthodox Jewry , that is the generality of orthodox Jews by this I wish to bring out that our teaching is that there is only one authentic brand of Judaism, the religion, as has been taught and handed down through the generations however there are various grades shall we say of adherence among Jews as regards to our religion regretfully and what I wish to do is talk to you in the name of orthodox Jews. What is an orthodox Jew? An orthodox Jew, is a Jew who endeavours to live his life completely in accordance with the Jewish religion and what is important today is that the Jewish religion and the Jewish belief absolutely forbids Zionism both on grounds of religious belief and on grounds of Jewish religious values of humanitarianism as I hope to explain.

Now even if you see and hear on the media what appear to be orthodox Jews supporting Zionism, as I will explain their approach is an aberration and a distortion of Judaism it is an absolute departure from the teaching that has been handed down to us through the generations, Zionism has the ideal and has always dreamt of imposing a secular but sectarian state over the heads of the Palestinians the indigenous population and it is this aim which has resulted in the terrible confrontation which has cost so many lives both Palestinian and Jewish with no end in sight unless there is a very radical change

A brief look at the Jewish religious belief point of view, our belief, our teaching is that we were given our [Hebrew] as its called and it has been taught to us through the generations by our great religious leaders and against this I want to have a brief look at the history of Zionism; how it developed and what are its aims. Now our religion is for us a total way of life showing us how to live a life in our service of the almighty, it affects every aspect of our life from the cradle to the grave we are taught that it was revealed to us by divine revelation as described in the bible some three and a half thousand years ago and that is when the Jewish people came into being. All our religious requirements; practical and philosophical are set out in the Torah and the Torah complies with the Bible the Old Testament and the vast oral teaching which has been handed down to us through the generations. I think it's relevant for you to understand also that Judaism does not have a missionary ideal we do not expect the whole world to adopt the Jewish religion. If one differentiates between the Jewish belief i.e. the belief in one god and the Jewish religion i.e. the practical requirements of the Jewish religion one can say that we would hope the whole world would have the belief in a god, which they generally do but which is being expanded to other religions where as we are taught that the Jewish practical religion is a requirement only for the Jews now as mentioned earlier, our religion is a total way of life covering every aspect of our life now one area and only one area of our religion our belief is that subject to certain conditions we would be given a land "the holy land" now known as Palestine in which to live and carry out various aspects of our service of the almighty. A said number of conditions, the conditions of our being granted this land were basically that we had to maintain the highest of moral, ethical, and religious standards; now it is history that the Jewish people did have the land for approximately the first one thousand five hundred years of their existence however regretfully the conditions were not fulfilled to the required degree and the Jews were exiled from this land and what has followed is that for the last two thousand years or so the Jewish people have been in a state of exile which is decreed by the almighty because they didn't maintain the standards expected of them. Now all this was and is foretold in our torah this state of exile is a situation that exists right up to the present day and the crux of the matter is that it is a basic part of our belief to except willingly and with humility that the heavenly decree of exile and not to try and fight against it or end it by our own hands to do so would constitute a rebellion against the wishes of the almighty.

Before I go any further I wish to point out something else which is also very basic to understanding the difference between Judaism and Zionism and that is that the orthodox Jewish concept of nation is very different to the concept of nationhood held by most people. Most peoples understand a nation to be a specific people living in a specific land. The English live in England the French in France and so on, the land is essential for the identity of the nation, the orthodox Jewish concept of nation however is different, it's a specific people with a specific religion and belief, it's the religion that establishes the national identity whether they have a land or not, the land is immaterial to the Jewish national identity. And this is born out if you think about it by the fact that the Jewish nation has been without a land for 2000 years but as long as they retained their religion they retained their identity.

So in practical terms then, we've maintained our identity by virtue of our attachment to our religion but…we are in exile we are taught that exile means for us this is our teaching, firstly that Jews must be loyal subjects of the countries in which they live and not attempt to rule over the established indigenous populations of those country. Our task is to remain politically neutral and not to impose demands, secondly we may not also part from our belief and we may not attempt to set up a state of our own in Palestine this would apply even if the land would be unoccupied as the early Zionists claimed that it was unoccupied, falsely of course but even if it was so we would be forbidden to set up our own state and it certainly applies when as is the case that there is an existing indigenous population, and this is what we have to understand; this prohibition on us is a basic part of our teaching and we are forsworn not to contravene it and we are also warned of dire consequences of doing so. This is what has been taught to us through the generations, from the religious belief point of view. Now let's consider the Zionist movement, this was founded approximately 100 years ago mostly by secular people who were discarding their religion but still retained what they considered as the stigma of being Jews in exile, they considered that our state of exile was due to our subservient attitude - what they called the 'golas mentality', 'golas' (the Hebrew word for exile) – and not by divine decree. They wanted to throw off the constraints of exile and to try and establish a new form of secular Jewish identity, not religion based but land based; based on the typical emotion driven, secular, nationalistic outlook similar to most other nations. Their policy had as its centrepiece the aim of setting up a specifically Jewish but secular state in Palestine, but what they were doing was forging a new kind of Jew, in fact not a Jew at all but something called a Zionist which is a different thing all together, so this Zionist movement was a complete abandonment of our religious teachings and faith in general and also an abandonment of our approach to our state of exile and our attitudes to the peoples among whom we lived. So the practical outcome of Zionism in the form of the state of Israel is completely alien to Judaism and the Jewish faith. In fact it may be of interest to know that the very name Israel was originally meant to denote the children of Israel i.e. the Jewish people, that name was usurped by the Zionists for popularistic reasons and for this reason many orthodox Jews avoid referring to the Zionist state by the name Israel. So it follows that from the belief point of view Jews have no right to rule today in Palestine and it is relevant, that from our approach that we have no right to rule in any of Palestine, ruling out the political so called "two state solution".

A further vital point is that the ideology of Zionism does not rely on divine providence but takes the law into its own hands and tries to force the outcome with their own force and form a state, and this is completely contrary to the approach of the matter of exile which our Torah requires us to adopt as handed down to us by our religious teachers. Now that's from the religious belief point of view now let's consider the Jewish religious values of humanitarianism and as I mentioned earlier this is I think the common denominator between all religions. The Zionist ideology was and is the force to form a state irrespective of the cost in life and property to anyone who stands in the way. So we have a fact that in order to achieve an ill-conceived nationalistic ambition, a shocking contravention of Jewish religious values of humanitarian justice was committed by the Zionists in setting up an illegitimate regime in Palestine completely against the wishes of the established population, the Palestinians depriving them of their self determination in the land they'd lived in for centuries and which almost inevitably had to be based on large scale theft and loss of life. The religious view is that one must have compassion and consideration for one's fellow man. Depriving a people of their home and country is totally contrary to this requirement. So there you have the two approaches, Zionist and orthodox Jewish. Most orthodox Jews accept the Neturei Karta view to the extent, this might be of interest to you, of course when I say orthodox Jews there are various shades of orthodox Jews but as a sort of basic guideline, Jews who look like me. Most orthodox Jews accept the Neturei Karta view to the extent that they do not agree in principle to the existence of the Zionist state and wouldn't shed a tear if it came to an end, although it has to be admitted that there are a range of opinions as to how to deal with the fact that for the time being the Zionist state of Israel does exist. And these opinions range from positive to operational, to pragmatic acceptance, to total opposition in every way, the latter of which being the Neturei Karta approach.

There is an additional Zionist phenomenon which I referred to briefly before and that is the religious Zionist. Now these are people who claim to be faithful to the Jewish religion but they have been influenced by the Zionist, secular, nationalistic philosophy and they have added a new dimension to Judaism and this is Zionism, which is the aim of setting up now and expanding a state in Palestine, they have added this, they have bolted this on to Judaism. I call it Judaism Plus. They claim that this is inherent to the Jewish religion, but the fact is as explained earlier and is clear to every unbiased student of the Jewish religion that this is absolutely contrary to the teachings of our great religious teachers as handed down to us through the generations. And from the humanitarian point of view, the religious Zionist ideology too is to simply force their aim irrespective of the cost of life or property of anyone who stands in their way, and this is all the more shocking as it is done in the name of religion. Whereas in reality, in reality, there is a totally contrary requirement of our religion, and that is to treat all peoples with compassion.

So to sum up, according to the Torah and the Jewish faith, the present Palestinian / Arab claim to rule Palestine is right and just, the Zionist claim is wrong and criminal. Our attitude to Israel has to be that the whole concept is flawed and illegitimate. But there is one more problem, and that is that the Zionist has made a tremendous impact on a large proportion of the Jewish people. And have in fact made themselves appear as the representatives and spokespeople of all Jews, thus with their actions arousing animosity against the Jews. And then those who harbour this animosity are accused of anti-Semitism. Zionism has ensnared and entrapped, regretfully a large section of the Jewish nation. In order to liberate ourselves from this entrapment, it has to be made abundantly clear that Zionism is not Judaism. Zionism, Zionists cannot speak in the name of Jews. Zionists may have been born as Jews, but to be a

Jew also requires adherence to the Jewish belief and religion. Opposition of Zionism and its crimes do not imply hatred of Jews or anti-Semitism. On the contrary, Zionism itself and its thieves are the biggest threat to Jews and Judaism, and are the biggest cause of anti-Semitism, or so-called anti-Semitism, in the world today. I say so-called because, thankfully the old fashioned, that there has been over the centuries, what I called the old fashioned bigoted form of anti-Semitist, thank Semitism, thankfully, since the Second World War, that has become almost non-existent I believe. But what has grown has been an anti, an anti-fearing against, what is, against the Zionist way of dealing with things.

My friends a central part of theology and religion is prayer. We pray for an end to bloodshed, and an end to the suffering of all innocent people, Jew and non-Jew alike worldwide.

I'd like to finish with the following words. We would wish to tell the people, especially our Arab neighbours, that there is no hatred or animosity between Jew and Arab. We would wish to live together as friends and neighbours as we have done so mostly over hundreds even thousands of years in all the Arab countries. In fact, over the years it is a historical fact, that when there was terrible persecution in Europe, the countries of refuge, were Arab and Muslim countries. And it was only the advent of Zionist and Zionism that upset this age old relationship. We are waiting for the annulment of Zionism, and the total, hopefully peaceful, dismantlement of the Zionist regime, which would bring about the end of the suffering of the Palestinian people. We would welcome the opportunity to dwell in peace in the Holy Land, under a rule which is entirely in accordance with the wishes and aspirations of the Palestinian people. May we soon know it the time, when all mankind would be at peace with each other. Thank you.

The Most Egregious Crime in Modern History: Palestinian Displacement

May El-Khansa

"Marsad" Association for Human Rights, Beirut

Abstract

Advocating for the right of return for Palestinian refugees to be effected by the international community and compensation to be provided, the author suggests that anything less would b e a failure to acknowledge the scale of the crisis and would undermine attempts at security and stabilization in the region.

The history of the displacement is summarised, and three key factors regarding the failure to implement international resolutions are discussed, namely: the ideological role of Zionism in perpetuating a neo-colonialist project; the fear, on the part of Palestinian advocates of transforming the discourse on Palestine from a political one to a humanitarian one; and a failure on the part of the international community to understand international legal provisos regarding refugees and / or a failure to implement them.

During the first conflict between the Arabs and Israel which arose in 1948, Israel occupied 77.4% of the Palestinian territory and forced 800 thousand Palestinians to migrate out of their own land. These were so far displaced to other regions in Palestine such as the West Bank and Gaza Strip or to the adjoining Arab countries like Jordan, Syria, Lebanon, Egypt, and Iraq. Later on, with the outbreak of the 1967 war between the Arabs and Israel, the Zionist government occupied the other Palestine territory forcing a great number of Palestinians who had been living in the West Bank and Gaza Strip to leave for Jordan.

Although the problem of the Palestinian refugees started approximately a quarter of a century ago, it remains the most important and vital problem which threatens, generally, the international peace and security and, particularly, the regional security in the Middle East. Therefore, the plight of refugees deserves of course to be one of the most foremost interests of the Arabs and the Islamic world.

In fact, the displacement of the Palestinian people from their homeland by the Zionist represents mostly an egregious crime in the modern history; a minority of foreign people had attacked the majority expatriating them from their houses and altering, on purpose and with prior plan, the architectural and demographic structure, under the political, military and financial support of the occidental States and the World Zionist Organization.

Resisting against the violence of the war, and of the numerous terrestrial and air raids against the displaced Palestinians and despite of the occupation, 88% of the Palestinian population is still living in the Arab territory; the majority of whom lives in the neighbouring countries, almost 46% of them refuse to leave their homeland, and 42% are dispersed in the adjoining Arab countries. As to the other 12%, i.e. one million citizens, half of them live in the other Arab countries and the others immigrated to Europe and America. It is important to notice that all these people are highly qualified, educated and skilled; this fact has allowed them to reach high ranking positions in these countries.

In 1948, the Zionist forces had pushed under arm threats the inhabitants of 530 cities, villages and tribes to leave their houses and occupied again an area of 18.6 dunnums (18600 million sq/m), i.e. 92% of Palestine total area, perpetrating more than 35 massacres to facilitate the domination over the whole country. Moreover, the latest statistics have shown that 89% of villages had been displaced due to Zionist military acts, 10% due to the psyche war (the method of frightening and terrifying), and only 1% have left according to the inhabitants decision, but all of them reclaim now and insist on the right of return.

Most of the settlement projects and the political, regional and international compromises which were dated from a long time ago and were over passed or those that were still put forward on the negotiation table failed to neglect the cause of the Palestinian refugees or to underestimate its importance because coming to a fair legal solution seems very urgent particularly when the Palestinian populations arrived to, due to their national and popular movement, defeating all the attempts of nationalization which aims at expatriating the Palestinians from their homeland. They also overthrew all the trials to oppress the right of return by referring to the resolution n°194 of the international legitimacy. However, with the serious insistence on the resistance and the reinforcement of their geographic and political existence, the Palestinians prove day by day real perseverance and confirm that the Palestinian matter is still a living one that raises debates in the International Community and in its relevant institutions and that it will stay alive in the conscience of all the free countries that refuse ignominy and injustice. Hence, the displaced Palestinians "Shatat" claim further the implementation of resolution n°194 which guarantees the Palestinian refugees' right of return and the instant application of resolution n°237 which stipulates the return of the migrating Palestinians who are frustrated from their rights and are subjected to the Israeli arbitrary, oppressive procedures and to the policy of evacuation adopted by Israel aiming at evacuating the land from their legal and original owners.

In view of the settlement projects that try to solve the conflict between the Palestinians and Israelis, many versions have been talked about as a fair solution to the problem of the Palestinian refugees with disregard to the international resolutions 194 and 237. Moreover, Israel has conditioned the omission of the right of return as the base to the end of the Arab-Israeli struggle and the establishment of an independent Palestinian State, in an attempt to shirk from the Israeli government's legal and moral responsibility toward the plight of the Palestinian refugees' expatriation and the lands and property expropriation, transferring all of them to the Zionist bands in order to build the basic structure of the Israeli occupation and State.

Under the international resolution n° 194, the establishment of an independent Palestinian state in the occupied territory of 1967 does not represent a prejudice to the right of return which won't be given up under any pressure. Thus, according to the independence declaration, Palestine is "a State for all the Palestinians wherever they are, where they developed their national identity and enjoy the equal rights". In reality, this establishment and the incorporation of the complete sovereignty on the land of Palestine will raise the national identity, the Palestinian existence and the historical rights and will enhance the continuous struggle for the implementation of the right of return by clinging to this right and confirming the compliance with resolution n° 194, plus exerting pressures on the Zionist government to respect the implementation of the above-mentioned resolution.

In addition, such procedures will enforce also the role of the United Nations on the problem of Palestinian refugees and the maintenance of the right of return in its resolutions as a personal right, in principal, that cannot be subjected to replacement in any convention or treaty and cannot be diminished by the establishment of the Palestinian Independent State.

Furthermore, this right represents a collective national right that concerns the Palestinian citizens as well as the refugees. It constitutes also a civil right that imposes the restoration of property, a political right that requires the establishment of citizenship, a national right for being one of the bases that incarnates the right of self determination for the Palestinians to constitute their own independent country and to come back home with regards to both the rights of return and compensation.

Although the world wide, international and Arab support to the refugees' rights of return and compensation, as individual and collective rights guaranteed by the international law and the United Nations resolutions, the International Community has failed until now to take serious and effective steps towards this internationally recognized right, while all over the world the international community has solved similar problems in different places where populations were subjected to racial cleansing policies, expatriation and eradication. For instance, the International Community has returned the refugees of Vietnam, Guatemala, Salvador, Rwanda, Croatia, Bosnia and Kosovo to their countries, but it does not move to bring back to the Palestinians their right in recuperating what Israel has taken from them and to help them return to their country.

The international community has instead of this called the two unequal parties, the Palestinian and Zionist occupation, to a "peace process", instead of applying the international laws, the United Nations resolutions and the rules of general justice applicable in other regions of the world.

Worth mentioning that the last two decades of the 20th century witnessed the return of millions of refugees to their homes in Africa; South Africa, Namibia, Mozambique and other African countries, to many countries in Asia; in middle Asia and in South East Asia and finally the return of custodian refugees to their cities and villages due the international military interference, known today by 'humanity interference'. Though the case of the Palestinian refugees represents one of the oldest and most dangerous matters in the world, it remains unsolved. In spite of being the only conflict to have gotten obvious UN resolutions on their right of return, the Palestinian refugees are the only ones in the world who didn't benefit from the positive developments that occurred in the planet and helped millions of refugees to regain their homelands. This fact can be referred to three factors:

1- The Zionist ideology of settlement and the annexation of all the Palestinian territory built on Zionist colonial and ideological basis and incorporated by the expatriation of the Palestinians from their lands by different means and the resettlement of other foreign population. Then, the hostile Israeli policy, supported by the biggest colonial countries, comes to refuse the admission of the Palestinian refugees matter and to deny their legal right in the voluntary return.

2- The Palestinian authorities' fear of the alteration of the Palestinian matter's character, transforming it into a humanitarian matter and depriving it from the political character, was behind the lack of concentration on the refugee matter as an independent one. However, this cause seems to be disintegrated from the purposes and the fields of the other conflict matters, a case that retains its own and special mechanisms, laws and dimensions. Therefore, such a plight should be turned into a major political and human case which exerts pressures on the States, responsible for the refugees' tragedy, and on the International Community conscience pushing it to mobilize.

As a result of the ineffective dealing with the refugees' plight, the matter has been placed at the end of national priorities instead of being the most important of them all and was replaced by intensive slogans with high rank. However, this position was not more than a baseless illusion; the importance is the refugees' return no matter if this took place under political or human slogans. In fact, the return of any group of refugees would be able to protect the territory, to reduce our endurances and to approach the achievement of the victory. Still our primordial purpose is to let the world know how important the refugee matter is, and that the existence of such a problem threatens the stability and the security in the region.

3- The ignorance of the international system on the refugees' protection, its mechanism, its legal document and how to deal with it. Therefore, the elimination of the Palestinian refugees from such a system becomes possible and decisive, a decision that was stipulated in paragraph (d) article 1 of the 1951 Geneva Convention relating to the Status of Refugees. Worth mentioning that the Egyptian and Iraqi delegated ministers had voted in favour of this elimination! No one knows if this resulted from ignorance or collusion, but it is quit clear that the Arab countries had voted before in 1948 negatively to the resolution n°194 that stipulated in its paragraph 11 the necessity of return of the Palestinian refugees and the payment of compensation for loss of property and damages. So the Palestinians were the only group to be out of this system that takes the responsibility to protect the refugees in the countries where they lived and helped some of them to find their way home.

Besides, the ignorance and the wrong estimation of the value of the refugee problem in our conflict with Israel, to its international dimensions, and to the lack of experience and the inability to control the refugees struggle with all its characteristics, factors, dimensions, and specific laws, added to the silence of Arab countries, ended with the withdrawal of the refugees return slogan from the international instruments those things that have facilitated the mission of Israel who replace the slogan of the refugees' return with the slogan of the Jews' return to the promised land. And in order to facilitate a comparison between the way we deal with the case of refugees and the ways that Israel follows to delude international public opinion, the World Jewish Organization (Zionist lobby) has issued a card or a sticker which holds the picture of Einstein on which they jetted down one word "the refugee".

But what hurts the most and excites the rage isn't the fact of the ignorance of the political and factional authorities, the jurists and diplomatists in international system relating to the protection of refugees only, but the fact that after fifty years of displacement and neglect of the Palestinian refugees matter, there are some who insist on ignoring and hiding the truth from others. The case is no more a political one neither a human cause that may stimulate the public opinion to take serious steps in order to put an end to this huge human injustice, and all this is supported by the position of the United States administration that stands against the return resolution and supports its ally, Israel, to wipe out the traces of the cause.

So, the matter of the Palestinian refugees has arisen and becomes the essence of the conflict that marked all the phases of the Palestinian plight which remains the most unsolved dimension in spite of all the trials aiming at finding a just settlement. Accordingly, giving a fair and global solution under international legitimacy to implement the right of return and compensation seems to be the first step on the way to securitize and stabilize the region and the main condition to solve all the other cases.

PART THREE:

The Right to Resist

This section sets out the theological arguments in Christianity and Islam. Rima Fakhry looks at Islamic concepts of freedom and sets out how freedoms usurped can be regained within an Islamic paradigm. She uses the experiences of the Lebanese resistance and the Palestinian *intifada* to elaborate on these concepts.

Ghada Ramahi takes the idea of resistance as a God-given right back to Islamic concepts of Haq i.e. truth and right. Contrasting this with the current lexicon of rights the genesis of which comes from a state system that self-appointed itself the authority to delegate rights, Ramahi argues that regardless of what rights are thus assigned, the right to resist is inherent. This immanence of the right to resist is God-given to all humans and when people are oppressed to extremes – regardless of who they are and whomsoever oppresses them - this right is one that many will feel justified in fulfilling.

Archimandrite Attallah Hanna outlines the nature of Christian Muslim solidarity and the shared experience of oppression. He highlights the commonality not only of experience but the theology of liberation, and the duty upon Christians as part of their faith, to resist oppression. He argues that implementation by the faith communities of this right not just locally but globally, would resolve the Palestinian struggle.

Towards a New Theology for Freedom: The Effects on Palestine

Rima Fakhry

Political Council, Hizbullah, Lebanon

Abstract

The author sets about defining freedom in the Islamic view, and ways of retaining the freedom usurped by oppressors. She contextualises them within the framework of Lebanese and Palestinian experience.

The author examines the factors that forced the Lebanese and Palestinian nations to choose military resistance, discussing Zionist identity, as well as an exposition of the resistance and Intifada outcomes including the: success of Lebanese resistance; effects of the Palestinian Intifada; deterioration of the economic basis of the Zionist state; human casualties; and the shaking of the military ideology for the Israeli Army.

In The Name Of Allah

Introduction:

In order to confront the Israeli aggression on land, man, and integrity, the great thoughtful resistance of Lebanon based its principles on faith in God and on commitment to the real Muhammadian Islam has been put into action since 1982, and all views around the world now are turning their faces to the resistance after proving its success and its effectiveness in the battlefield.

Who are these people? What is their religious and thinking background?

Why are they ready to offer all these sacrifices to get back freedom and integrity?

Hardly had the interrogators quenched their wonderment, when soon the Intifada of Palestine lit the sky of liberators based on faith in God and devoted to Islam's principles.

Many years have passed and our new era is one where oppression and injustice have spread all over the earth and where Lebanon and Palestine have presented two prominent examples of resistance.

A dignified successful vision of freedom which has given us victory and triumph can only be made through religion and belief in God, his laws, and principles.

In this debate, I'll show briefly the unique experience of the resistance, and state some reasons that help it achieve success and free the Lebanese and Palestinian people. We greatly hope that this resistance be a good example for all oppressed people to follow. And we hope to see justice spread all over the globe.

Defining Freedom According to the Islamic Perspective:

God has created humans with different natural potentials and motives among which his unlimited desire is to be totally free from any restraint. As a result, every being searches endlessly for his freedom within the moral scope by dispelling all the impediments that may block his potential and willingness to precede to the wide infinite heavenly universe. Not only does the human look for freedom within the moral scope but also within the social one. So he tries to wipe out all the obstructions that could stand in his way from having comfort and luxury. This goes on with his scope of freedom in Fukih, history, and rightfulness. Though freedom differs in its scope and applications, it still has one definition in different areas. The linguistic and knowledgeable definition of freedom is the same which means the absence of captivity and restriction. Such definition was recurrently used in the Islamic literature. In fact, there are firm beliefs in the Islamic enactment that says freedom lies in the origin of human life until slavery is confessed or accepted. Since religion has the priority in our life over freedom, it should direct and define freedom.

Imam Ali (p.b.u.h.) said:

> **"Oh, people, Adam has not given birth to a slave**
> **male or female, but all people are free."** [i]

This saying explains that freedom **is a real rooted truth of the humanity**, and every individual is born with the right to live freely irrespective of his\her race, religion or sect. Moreover, any person who reviews Quraan verses and holy sayings for the prophets and Imams will find that it is full of freedom's talking. These verses and sayings considered freedom as:

-_Islam's endowment, **"Allah has sent his servant testimonial verses to lead you from darkness into light."** [ii]

- A divine bless and duty, **""freedom is a heavenly trust that God has specifically given to us."** (Imam Khomaini p.b.) [iii]

-_An indispensable condition for all types of modernization and development. There is no way for any oppressed people to be civilized, developed or modern without freedom.

Therefore, this affinity, desire, and nostalgia towards freedom exists in every human being. But, unjust and haughty leaders try to chain this desire for they are afraid of having free men in society, so they try to usurp all kinds of freedom to be able to control the resources and potentials of all peoples and countries.

Islam at every time speaks of an obvious rule which is **"God has entrusted Adam's son to do all his affairs unless he humiliates himself."** [iv]

It is forbidden for Man to accept degradation and slavery for his fellow man, but it is his wajib to do all his best to regain freedom for his fellow man.

> **"All free men in the world must know that they have to offer a valuable price for Liberty and independence in case they wanted to stand bondless from any power or great nation." Imam Khomeini (p.b.u.h.)** [v]

-_Therefore, in Islam there are unchangeable facts that could be summarized as following:
- Man is free.
- It is an obligatory duty to retain freedom and preserve it in case it is usurped.
- Every individual has to do his best to guard his freedom within what Islamic Shariaa conforms to him.

The Possible Means that Could be Used to Restore Usurped Freedom.

According to what has been mentioned, Man has to use any method or style that conforms with the Shariaa in order to regain the lost freedom. After looking back at the long historical experience of different peoples all over the world, we come to deduce 2 kinds of ways to restore freedom. The first is negotiations and diplomacy, and the second is the resistance. This resistance has many levels that starts with rejecting to deal with the enemy to civil protesting until it reaches its higher stage as a military resistance. The people of a country, circumstances, the enemy and other considerations determine what type of resistance to choose.

Our Experience in Lebanon and Palestine as a Real Example

First since freedom is a right for every community and individual, second since each person must do their best to restore the usurped freedom, and third since gaining freedom is restricted to negotiations and diplomacy or resistance with all its levels, two experiences shone out as representatives of present-day resistance. These experiences are the Lebanese resistance and the Palestinian Intifada. We have chosen these two sample experiences to investigate because of the common grounds between them. Both face the same enemy, Zionism, and the two countries have defended their freedom in many ways.

First: Palestine

The Zionists occupied Palestine in 1948 and announced the name of their country. Since then, they have started to commit massacres against Palestinians and to prosecute mass expulsion of the natives towards the nearby countries, Lebanon, Jordon, Syria and Egypt. Since that time until now, the Arabs and the Palestinians have used the diplomatic style, negotiations, with the help of the International Security Council. The Palestinian case was considered one of the complicated issues in that it was scheduled at the top of the work lists of the United States President and other European presidents. The International Security Council issued tens of resolutions about Palestine and Palestinian people; some of which ask Israel to withdraw from some land that had been occupied or what is known as 1967 lands, while some other resolutions ask for the right of the Palestinian to come home. However, since 1948 and until our day, Palestine is still occupied and Israel did not withdraw even from 1967 lands adding to the refugees who are dispersed and who are living in refugee camps in the neighbouring countries.

Therefore, after 57 years of diplomatic work, the Palestinian people have not been liberated yet, and all of us know their pain and tragedy and I wish that I had a chance to talk about it. Different from diplomacy, the Palestinians had undergone a weaponry intifada experience. The first intifada forced the Zionists to start negotiating with the Palestinians and other Arab countries. Of course, that was likely to be a manoeuvre that sought more time and to disperse powers, so the Zionists were the winners as the first intifada stopped and they prepared themselves again.

In contrast, the second intifada still exerts pressure on the Israeli entity and forces it to admit to withdrawal from Gaza, according to Sharon's plan, even if this is not what Palestinians look for. (Furthermore there would be presentations of some facts concerning the effects of the intifada on the Zionist entity).

Second: Lebanon

Since the occupation of Palestine by the Zionist, the Lebanese land, people and sovereignty have been exposed to attacks. Because of the Zionistic massacres in all towns and villages, thousand of martyrs died, adding to the absence of secure feelings by the Lebanese citizens not forgetting the recurrent materialistic losses such as agricultural lands, roads, water dams and other public plants. With each attack the Lebanese government used to hand in a complaint for the Security Council that in turn issued condemnatory resolutions against the attacks and called to give it up. Yet all fell on a deaf ear. This continued until the Zionist occupied a great part of the Lebanese land and in 1982 they occupied the capital Beirut. Hence, the 425 Resolution was enacted and it states that the Zionist entity must withdraw from Lebanon up to the international territories. Since 1982 and up until 2000, this resolution was just a discourse and was not attended to by the Zionists. 18 years passed and the Zionists were still occupying our land, meanwhile the international resolutions were issued one after the other.

So What Expelled the Zionists from Lebanon?

It is crystal clear and all of us know very well that the military resistance did, a fact admitted by the Zionists themselves.

What Urged the Lebanese and the Palestinian People to Choose Military Resistance?

Simply, it is experience lived by both people on one hand, and the Zionist identity on the other.

The Zionist Identity:

Since its existence and until now, the Zionist identity is based on some superstitious and fabricated racist set of beliefs, to run its Zionist project in Palestine and the world. They consider themselves "the chosen nation" that God has chosen specifically from all other people to be the leaders of others and enslave them. Thus, according to these beliefs, all others are worthless people unless they offer the chosen nation some services. That is why you would see them despising all other religions and considering themselves to have the right to do anything for their interest and benefit. When the Zionists try to defend their forcible seizure of the Palestinian land, they deal with the Palestinian people as if they are nonsensical and primitive who don't deserve to have a country. As an example, here are some words from the Zionist researcher "Israel El Dad" that talk about his denial of the Palestinian people: "**Could there be a kind of comparison between the rich Zionistic existence and the Palestinian nation? Who are the Palestinians? What is this nation? What are its distinctive and mental features?**" [vi] Therefore, such a haughty arrogant figure who is not ready to acknowledge others and living in a world were only might exists and international resolutions disappear, in such a world and facing such an enemy, which way could the sensible people choose to restore their freedom?

An Analytical Approach to the Resistance and Intifada Results.

The military resistance had left wide positive results on the struggle movement with the Zionist enemy, noted by the great sacrifices offered in both Lebanon and Palestine.

- The resistance in Lebanon generated freedom and prosperity.

The resistance was able, even before the "Israeli" withdrawal from the country's land, to enforce a panic equation on this enemy in which the "Israeli" army had to guard against before undertaking any attack against the Lebanese free land. And this equation was crystallized by what was named as "April's Arrangement", in which the "Israeli enemy was prevented from inflicting any attack on any civil site at the risk of attacking the Israeli settlements in north occupied Palestine.

Such panic equation that was enforced by the resistance in Lebanon protected Lebanese civil people and economy, tourism and infrastructure. And while Lebanon was an unsafe place especially for foreign tourists, because of the "Israeli" invasion on its land and facilities, and of the incessant offences, it turned out to be the safest place among the countries. Also, it attracted one million tourists in the last year. In addition to that there was an increase in the national and international investments rates, and the rebuilding of its infrastructure in most of its land.

As a summary, it could be said that the resistance weapon confronting such a haughty enemy as the Zionist refreshed all Lebanese sectors and its installation in Lebanon offered more than 1400 fighter martyrs during the jihad period, thousands of the civil martyrs, and huge economic and developmental destruction. But the result was the withdrawal of the enemy from its land. Therefore, due to the Lebanese example, the prestige of the miracle army that was never ever defeated was ended. And the pieces of evidence are many. Let's notice some of the Israeli phrases about their way of dealing with the Lebanese trouble as presented in their own press.

-_"We are defeated in the war in Lebanon. This is how Lebanon conquered us deeply." (Haa'rets 18\2\2000)

-_"We lost this war in Lebanon. It's easy to feel the panic and depression of the soldiers' families." (Haa'rets 15\2\2000)

The effects of the Palestinian Intifada :

The Palestinian Intifada has not come to an end yet, however, I find it necessary to present some statistics that show the positive effects of the Pal. Intif along the path of liberating both the land and the men/women from the Israeli occupation (the Intifada revived as a result to the failure of all the diplomatic talks and negotiations).

1- Deterioration of the economic components in the Zionist Entity :[vii]

The outbreak of the Palestinian Intifada, by the end of Septenmber 2000, led to a confusion in the economic, financial, and monetary policies in Israel, hence the cost of occupation increased.

- The economic growth rate decreased from 6% to 2%. This affected the income of the Zionist settlers by decreasing their share of the annual GDP by 3% (between 2000 of 2002).
- In the construction and building sector, construction decreased by 10.5% in 2001 which led to the increase of unemployment from 8.4% in the year 2000 to 11% in 2003.
- The effects of the Intifada were seen clearly as the tourist facilities closed down and the number of tourists decreased greatly.
As a result tourism returns decreased by 7 billion $ in the 90's to 500 million $ in 2003.

We would like to mention an assessment given by the vice-president of the research department at the "Bank of Israil" Michael Streetenky who said: "In terms of dollors, the Intifada costed us the loss of 23 billion $. A huge sum that overweighs the

American monetary aids and the budget decreases. Furthermore, every middle-income family lost 14.500$ over the last 3 years as a result of 'Al Intifada' ." [viii]

2- Human Losses

Al Aksa's Intifada witnessed a qualitative development. It developed both its operations and its weapons. Consequently this raised, the human and material losses on the enemy's behalf while it decreased the Palestinian sacrifices. Comparing the enemy's losses with those of the Palestinian people's sacrifices, we notice that between 29/9/2000 – 19/8/2003, The enemy lost :
711 casualties (militants and settlers)

5400 wounded (militants and settlers)

While the Palestinian martyrs were 170 martyrs among the militants in addition to hundreds of martyrs among the civilians (women – children, and elderly).

3- The military faith of the Israeli Army:

The most important consequence to the Palestinian Intifada was pushing the "Israeli military strategic premises" on which the Israeli security theory was built.
How did this become apparent ?
The military strategy of the Zionist entity supposed, until a few years ago, that they were capable of "**winning the battle without having to go through it**", based on a conviction that the Palestinians consider the Zionist army as a superior and strong enemy and that the Palestinians are dominated by fear, thus they will absolutely be defeated in no time .

The resistance's experience marvelously destroyed the legend of the "undefeatable army", to the extent that children started to make fun of that legend.

The act of resistance changed the rules of the game. Eventually, the Israeli army had to take several measures in the battle field.

Here are the most important changes:

1- The enemy had to forgo the principle of the striking first, because it proved futile against the resistance's operations .

2- The enemy had to defend "Israeli" from inside its territories and not from the outside for example :
- The Israeli army had to deploy intensively along the Northern border in fear of any penetration by the Islamic Resistance.
- "Almirsad (1) " plane sent by the Islamic Resistance twice to fly over the occupied Palestinian territories; thus, it challenged the Israeli arrogance and its high-tech

military technology. The resistance made the enemy helpless: unable to protect its air, unable to protect its borders, and unable to control the occupied territories.

- Taking extensive measures inside Telaviv to reduce the danger incurred by the Palestinian Resistance's operations.

3- A loud argument emerged assuring the need to look for new means to rebuild the Israeli deterrence power which dwindled as a result of the resistance's and Intifada's strikes. The most expressive quote that reflects that situation was made by one of the Israeli strategy experts,"**The deterrence's image of Israeli is doomed to vanish and the continuation of the Intifada makes this image deteriorate even more, and with every passing day Israel is belittled as it fails to stop the Intifada. This inability leaves us more vulnerable, more confused, and more susceptible to pressure an internal partitions.**"[ix]

4-The resistance proved the reality of its saying, "It is possible to overcome the qualitative superiority of the Israeli army in the battlefield. And it is possible to turn this superiority from a helping factor into a source of confusion that hinders the army's motion in the battlefield.

5- The resistance revealed the fragile side of the Israeli society, and it shed light on many of the discrepancies on the psychological and moral level.

6- The enemy admitted that the resistance imposed a new formula that counterbalanced the enemy's abilities in terms of deterrence and panic. So the Israelis assumed a defending position and they were obliged to abide by the conditions imposed in the battlefield.

Conclusion

In light of the above, the resistance proved effective in imposing a new formula of terror upon this arrogant enemy. An enemy who refuted all treaties, charters, and commitments. An enemy who proved to be disrespectful of the United Nations and its institutions as long as their resolutions did not meet the zionist's interests solely. Accordingly, scientific reasoning is the only means by which the Palestinians can regain their complete freedom, and by which they will achieve victory. And this was dictated in the human rights charter which acknowledged for all the peoples of the world the right to live freely on their land.

Moreover, any peoples who were deprived of the right to live freely are acknowledged the right to resist in order to regain their freedom. What has been accomplished so far motivates all those who are sincere to the subjugated and oppressed people to support the Palestinian people in their endurance and in their perseverance along the path of "aljihad". Maybe it's the end or at least the beginning of the end of this oppression and injustice.

And according to a saying by Amir Elmouminine Ali Ibn Abi Taleb (pbuh):
"There is life in your death as conquerors, and there is death in your life when you are conquered."

Genuine life is what all the fighters and martyrs of Palestine will achieve and true death afflicts the living defeatists and languids.

End Notes:

[i] – Alkafi – part 8-p.79
[ii] – Alhadid -9 / the Holy Koran
[iii] – Short words – p – 142
[iv] – Holly saying
[v] – Short words
[vi] – A trip Inside the Mind of an Israelian teacher and a researcher – p.9 – Bahith for studies .
[vii] – The effects of Intiada on the Zionist Entity, Baheth for studies, p.203
[viii] – Same reference – p.217 – Statisties for the period between 2000 and 2003
[ix] – Amniz Yair – "Politica" weekly publication – Octobre 1989

Who Gives the Right to Resist?

Ghada M. Ramahi

Researcher in History and Philosophy of Western and non-Western sciences, New York, USA.

Abstract

Contemporary state systems have appropriated the authority to delegate Rights to people.
As a result human rights have been reconstituted, modified, manipulated and delegated unjustly in the interest of political power.

At the 1st anniversary of the death of Shaikh Ahmed Yaseen & Dr Abdul Aziz Ranteecie (leader of Hamas) the question needs to be raised as to what makes educated men with significant earning potential take the difficult and treacherous path of a freedom fighter

Hizbullah, Islamic Jihad, Hamas etc are political players whose reality and political significance can not be denied.
We need to understand the driving force behind such organisations.

They are driven by an instinctive sense of injustice and an innate right to resist; just a child is driven by an innate but unarticulated sense of injustice when it has his/her toy snatched, taken or stolen. The child resistance in the form of tears, tantrums, fighting for the return of the toy is driven by instinct.

Islamically, through the language of Arabic, the word Haq is used to mean Right. Haq connote only just Rights and the word is derived form Absolute/Divine Haq—Allah. Hence one's Haq implies divinely bestowed 'Just Right'. Not every Right is a Haq but every Haq is Right. The Haq to resist is the driving force behind Hamas, Islamic Jihad, Hizbullah. Having the Haq to resist is to object to something that is unjustly being forced upon you.

In its attempt to reconstruct humanity, the contemporary state system has given itself the authority to delegate rights to inhabitants of the Earth. In the process, human rights were reconstituted, modified, invented and delegated unjustly. The result is a term which is very vague, elastic and quite subjective. Some rights are luxurious and frivolous while others are instinctive and essential for survival. One person's Right might be to get freshly cut flowers delivered every morning to decorate the table while having breakfast on the balcony of an exclusive apartment on the 39th floor of a high rise over looking the skyline of the city. While another person's right might be limited to securing clean running water and sanitized sewage system. One person's right might be to renew the car every year, whereas another person's right might be to simply exist!

Not only are reconstituted rights relative, but also manipulated and politically designed depending on ethnicity, nativity, race, sex, religion, language, natural resources, and other classification that fits the grand chessboard of the powers to be. So, the issue here is what constitutes a Right and who has the authority to define it and consequently delegate it.

In its capacity as a subsidiary to the contemporary state system, the United Nations became the arbiter of human rights. In fact, it presided over the production of the Universal Declaration of Human Rights. However, a minor problem emerged! The UN has never been an objective impartial arbiter. A stark example is Resolution 194, Article 11, which is supposedly the reference for "the right to return", According to Answer.com, "the resolution (actually only Article 11) has been increasingly quoted by the Arabs, who have interpreted it as a 'right of return' of the Palestinian refugees." So what is it about this article that is open to different interpretations?

The ambiguity of the wording of the first stipulation of the article calls for a closer examination. The paragraph is worded ambiguously without any specifications regarding who precisely has the "right to return", whereas the second stipulation specifies precisely who should be repatriated, resettled and compensated….. The Palestinians! Therefore, the vague first stipulation was not meant for the Palestinian refugees, rather for the Jews who should have the "right to return" since they were refugees in diasporas for the past 2000 years. This means that someone who had never belonged to the land of Palestine nor lived in it was considered as a refugee awarded the "right to return", whereas Palestinian who were uprooted from their homeland were, or actually are still, offered other alternatives apart from a return!

With this insight, one can understand why the state of Israel first welcomed the UN Resolution 194, article 11, and later continued to ignore it. Furthermore, UN resolutions are not obligations, rather recommendations AND are always open for different interpretations to the disadvantage of those who are on the receiving end. Having said the above, let's look at UN Resolution 194, Article 11 as it appeared on answer.com,

> "The General Assembly,
> Having considered further the situation in Palestine,
> [Articles 1 through 10 are listed]
>
> 11. Resolves that the refugees wishing to return to their homes and live at peace with their neighbours should be permitted to do so at the earliest practicable date, and that compensation should be paid for the property of those choosing not to return and for loss of or damage to property which, under principles of international law or in equity, should be made good by the Governments or authorities responsible;

Instructs the Conciliation Commission to facilitate the repatriation, resettlement and economic and social rehabilitation of the refugees and the payment of compensation and to maintain close relations with the Director of the United Nations Relief for Palestine Refugees and, through him, with the appropriate organs and agencies of the United Nations"

This past April while home in my comfy living room, I sat watching a segment of the evening news reporting on Hamas commemorating the first year anniversary of the martyrdom of Shaikh Ahmad Yaseen and Dr. Abdul Aziz Al Ranteecie. On the stage and behind the speakers, huge pictures of the martyred Hamas leaders hung. I counted them. They were ten: starting with Yahiya 'Ayyash all the way up to Abdel Aziz Al Ranteecie. For a few moments there, my thoughts transcended my identity as a Palestinian or in fact as any other nationality and I found myself asking in pure abstraction: what is it that made these men and such with their calibre of educational achievement choose this path for their lives? Why didn't they choose to get fancy jobs with their highly esteemed degrees? Why not brag about their career accomplishments and investment portfolios like others with similar technical qualifications? Why didn't they choose to sit in the negotiating seat and shake hands like other politicians? What differentiated them from some other men? What made them decide to live underground, not being able to walk casually on a street? These men are not just teenagers where some "fanatic leader had brainwashed them into enlisting in a radical movement" as a western political analyst once roared.

No matter on which side of the "wall" one might sit (and here I mean The WALL), and regardless of how one might view Hamas, Islamic Jihad and Hizbullah, no one can deny their presence. Their accomplishments are immensely impacting both sides of the "wall". They are major players and decisive factors in world politics. Classifying them as terrorist groups does not make them go away nor does assassinating their leaders weaken them. In the case of Hizbullah, they managed successfully to force the Israelis out of almost the entire southern part of Lebanon. Recently, both Hamas and Hizbullah "democratically" have won major elections. If this is so, then one must try, objectively if ever humanly possible, to fathom the driving force behind such groups.

Every one of us here remembers how we have felt when another kid had snatched our toy and wouldn't want to give it back. As very little ones, we didn't know or understand why we would get really upset and cry ... instinctively we knew that something was wrong, and that what belonged to us was taken away, it had been usurped "Someone took something that belongs to me". And the other kid was unjust and was not supposed to do that to me. To protest and to get our toy back, we did all we could expressing it in anger, cried very loud, kicked and did not accept any other toy for replacement. When we were forced to accept and given a replacement, we were never satisfied and kept our eyes fixed on what was taken away from us, and went after it when the first chance presented itself. Perhaps this was our first experience of injustice and resistance.

Now as an adult, I know that if another person came and by force kicked me out of my house and claimed it his, took my trees, my garden, my farm, my land, and took my whole country and claimed it as his, then he denies my identity and does not want me to even exist. When I react to all of these injustices, he classifies me according to his political agenda and gains. Using his own constructed world institutions, he tries to crush me by all possible means.

The feeling that we did not understand as children but acted upon is called one's right … it is an instinctive feeling that comes with the human make-up; it is part of the hardware. No body gave it to us, we were born with it. It runs with our blood.

Islamically speaking, in Arabic there is a very specific word that is used to mean Right. It is the word 'haq', with 'hoqook' for plural. Strictly, the word 'haq' connotes only a 'just Right'. This is so because the word 'haq' as Right is derived from the Absolute Haq, Allah the Almighty (swt). The Absolute Haq is also the root of the word 'Haqeeqah' which means the Absolute Truth. Haq is one of the Ninety Nine Divine Attributes. Hence, one's haq implies a divinely bestowed 'Just Right'. Unfortunately, lately in the Arab world the words haq and right have been confused and used interchangeably which has resulted in further alienation and massive confusion. Not every right is Haq, but every Haq is right. No language is necessary to know one's Haq, but plenty of it is needed to know one's rights. Haq cannot be understood mechanistically nor does it follow science, technology, economic growth, or tourism. Haq cannot be affected by any man made laws and regulations. Haq cannot be crushed by any military supremacy. No power can deny one's Haq but power can deny one's right. A world agency might decide some rights in favour of one over the other, but it does not make these rights just. Those who are unjustly awarded some rights on the expense of others will always know that they have cheated. The haq to resist defies negotiations, road maps and highly erected concrete walls. The haq to resist is the driving force behind Palestinian uprising, behind Hamas, Islamic Jihad and behind the strength of Hizbullah. It was the power that made the quadriplegic Shaikh Ahmad Yaseen resist and it is what makes the bare-chested Palestinian youth fight the Mercava with stones. It is what keeps Palestinian prisoners standing tall.

Having the haq to resist is to object actively to something that is unjustly forced upon you. It is to strive against something bad that is harming you, even when the super powers of the world don't think so. It is to remain firm against the action and effect of occupation and to withstand the aggression imposed on every aspect of your livelihood. And because haq is the essence of resistance, it is only the Almighty Absolute Haq that divinely instills in our psyche the notion of instinctive rights, so when one has the Haq to resist, one is delegated this right by the Almighty Allah (swt).

The Meaning of Peace and Making a Meaningful Peace

Archmandrite Attallah Hanna
as translated by Imam Muhammad Al-Asi

Greek Orthodox Patriarchate, Jerusalem

Abstract

Emphasising the nature of Jerusalem as the city of peace and brotherhood between three faiths, the presenter empahsises on the nature of Christian Muslim solidarity and the shared experience of oppression. He highlights the commonality not only of experience but the theology of liberation, and the duty upon Christians as part of their faith, to resist oppression. If such teachings were implemented, the presenter contends that the oppression of the Palestinians would be resolved.

First of all I would like to greet you, I am speaking to you in Jerusalem, I would also like to wish your conference success and thank you for giving me the opportunity to participate n this hopefully successful conference.

I am speaking to you from the center of Jerusalem to be specific from the church of the Holy Sepulchre. I wanted to be with you physically but due to the circumstances that is not possible so now it is this method that we are using, it is a communication via this a telephonic link from which I will be addressing you.

This city of Jerusalem is a city that is sacred to three religions it is supposed to be the city of peace and brotherhood, but regrettably it is the furthest it can be from peace and brotherhood and that is attributable to the Israeli occupation of the city and the infliction of untold misery and undue circumstances that are imposed upon the Palestinians in this city and in the occupied territory and wherever the Palestinians may happen to be.

I am addressing you not only in my capacity as a clergyman but also being that I am an Arab and a Palestinian who is speaking to you from the heart or the centre of this city and this homeland, a homeland in which Muslims and Christians live together being united or amalgamated by the same cause and the same destiny so to speak.

The Christians, we are not speaking about Christians only or Christian churches that are suffering from the circumstances and the conditions of the Israeli occupation rather we speak about the Christians and Muslims who are together without any discrimination living in similar circumstances as brothers suffering from the same occupation and working together as Christians and Muslims to try to do away with this occupation and try to build a Palestinian state with its capital being the city of Jerusalem.

We in our church offer our prayer for the sake of peace. We want a peace that envelopes the whole area, we want the stability of a peace but in order to have peace we must have justice and in order for us to have justice we have to eliminate oppression and injustice to make it possible to have the conditions of this peace that we speak about. The oppression and injustice is represented by the different sorts of aggressive action that is taken against us by the types of policies that winded up eliminating some of us. In order for us to speak of peace and to have peace we have to eliminate the psychological barriers above us; not only the physical barriers that exist here, we also need this to happen to feel the joy and to feel the word with a meaning of peace that we use.

In the name of the Christians and the Muslims we plead with you in the name of the common brotherhood that we have. We ask of your conference to present this just issue of Palestine and the Palestinians so that you may contribute to eliminating the oppression that we are experiencing here, we plead with you to show understanding to express this issue so that you may be able to become supportive of our Palestinian people, we are in need of you. We are in need of you to express the truth to express this just cause and to express what peace means in this context, we are in need of you for this objective of peace so that you may contribute and help us in this regard. We are in need of the freedom that you enjoy and that we are denied.

Christians in the world are expected according to the teachings of the Holy book to show support to those who are oppressed. This is an obligation to all Christians in the world which in our case would mean the end of occupation, we plead with the Christians in the world to show support and to offer aid to our oppressed Palestinian people so it becomes possible for them to break loose from the type of imprisonment and the type of occupation that we suffer from here in the Holy Land.

I believe, and I will wind down my presentation, that the Palestinian people have to be solved but in order for them to be solved there has to some issues that have to be solved accordingly. The first one is the issue of Jerusalem. Jerusalem has to be returned to its rightful people and it has to be liberated from its current condition. And number two, the refugees, the Palestinian refugees have the right, the inalienable right to return. There cannot be a Palestinian who is denied his home, and his homeland and the city that he comes from. All Palestinians have the right to return regardless of the expulsions that they have suffered during 1948 and 1967 and other dislocations that they are living in. It should be emphasised that this inalienable right to return to their home and their homeland.

At the end I would like to thank you for this opportunity, you gave me the opportunity to speak to you from Jerusalem and I hope and I pray that in the future it would be possible for you all to visit us here in Jerusalem. I greet you from Jerusalem, from Al Masjid al-Asqa, from the Church of the Holy Sepulchre, from all the churches, from all the institutions that are in this city and in this land and I pray for peace, for love and for brotherhood especially in this area during this time and thank you once again for this opportunity.

PART FOUR:

Conceptualising the Methods of Liberation

Advocating a solidarity between Israeli and Palestinian activists, Leah Tsemel calls for a relegitimsation of resistance within discourse around Palestine and the differentiation of this from terrorism. She argues for a recognition of the cat of survival of the Palestinian people as well as the solidarity shown by Israeli activists as essential to preventing the sociocide of the Palestinian people.

Imam Achmad Cassiem looks at conceptual framework of the Qur'an to define resistance per se and specifically with regard to Palestine, as Palestine in the Quran is entrusted to the Muslims. This trust (amanah) defines Muslim rights, obligations, methods and objectives in relation to Palestine. Cassiem argues that the primary objective of trustees is to serve the interest of Mankind, not of a particular socio-economic class, race, tribe or nation. Whilst he argues that resistance constitutes a law of nature and that this is endorsed in Islam, resistance is not sufficient to end or eradicate oppression. Using the Quranic verse, *"And why should ye not fight in the Cause of Allah and the oppressed" (Quran 4:75)*, Cassiem argues that participation in the process of liberation means to be committed to the oppressed.

Rev Steven Sizer presents the work of Liberation Theologian Naeem Ateek and the Sabeel Center in Palestine. Focussing on passive resistance, Sizer sets out the project within established understandings of liberation theology within a Christian context, and the primarily Catholic experience in South America, while reconceptualising that from an ecumenical Christian perspective.

Imam Muhammad Al-Asi argues that if the current pejorative conceptualisations relating to the terms Islamic fundamentalism, radical Islam etc could be neutralised, the purpose and project of those often ambiguously labelled would be redefined thus: that Islam is a theological ideology and an ideological theology compressed in one scripture. Its primary and principle concern is with Justice. The historical covenant of God's relationship with people is define not by race, but rather by the individual's conviction and principles. These convictions and principle are to be rooted in social justice, equity and equality. Thus the struggle for justice and against injustice forms the character of a sincere and committed Muslim.

Message to the Conference

Leah Tsemel

Human Rights Lawyer- Haifa

Abstract

Advocating a solidarity between Israeli and Palestinian activists, Leah Tsemel calls for a relegitimsation of resistance within discourse around Palestine and the differentiation of this from terrorism. Highlighting the struggles of inter alia: the parents and children who defy attempts at school closures by going to / sending their children to school; the elderly who refuse to accept the obstructions to their daily routine by Israeli forces; Israeli refuseniks and those from all backgrounds protesting the wall, Tsemel helps to reconceptualise acts of resistance as taking many forms, from violent struggle to the most mundane acts of daily survival. All of these she sees as essential to preventing the sociocide of the Palestinian people.

Since the American Revolution, more than two centuries ago, one has not only the right to resist oppression, but the **duty** to do so. The UN Charter, the Universal Declaration of Human Rights and the Geneva Conventions, have repeated this inalienable right to resist and to struggle for freedom and independence.

In the last few years, the massive use of the concept of "terrorism" has been intentionally used in order to reverse this basic humanistic and universal philosophy, and to de-legitimize the right to resist oppression. When Israeli Prime Minister, war-criminal Ariel Sharon claimed "Yasser Arafat is our Ben Laden", he intended to reverse the world-wide support to the legitimate struggle of the Palestinian people against occupation and colonialism, and to present the Israeli colonial war as a war of self-defense against terror. He is now trying to do the same with president Mahmud Abass.

Our first duty today is **to re-legitimate the right of resistance,** and to draw a dividing line with terrorism: terrorism is obviously not mass mobilization against occupation; it is neither armed struggle against occupation forces; terrorism is any attack against civilians, whether by a state using combat helicopters and missiles, or a young boy putting a bomb in a crowded bus. As such, terrorism has to be denounced and unequivocally rejected. Saying so, I want however to make a distinction between Major General Dan Halutz, the new Israeli chief of staff who, as commander of the Israeli air force, gave three years ago, the order to throw a one thousand kilo bomb on a populated area in Gaza, provoking the death of more than 10 innocent civilians, including children, and a young Palestinian from Balata refugee camp, who has lost his brother, seen his father humiliated in front of him, witnessed the destruction of tens of thousands of houses in his camp and finally decided to explode himself in a cafe in Tel Aviv. In both cases we are speaking of persons committing terrorist acts, but while the first one is undoubtedly a war criminal, the second one is a desperate freedom fighter using a criminal way to fight his legitimate struggle. This is why, as a human rights lawyer, I have no problem, whatsoever, to defend him.

The Palestinian people are resisting occupation, with demonstrations, with stones, with guns. But, in the present context, while the Israeli state target is to commit a real sociocide and to destroy the Palestinian society as a society, the most efficient resistance, the one which made the Israeli plan fail, is the day-to-day resistance of the mothers and the fathers, the pupils and the teachers, the municipal employees and the ambulance drivers who refuse to "return to the age of stone", if to use US General Westmoreland dream in Vietnam.

By sending their children to schools despite the dangers and the closure, Palestinian parents are resisters; by reaching the wounded people, despite the checkpoints, ambulance drivers and paramedics are resisters; by repairing, time after time, their destroyed towns, and not accepting to live in ruins, municipal employees are resisters. Crossing or by-passing the closure system, the checkpoints and the wall in order to visit an ill grand-mother and refusing to leave her in her loneliness is an act of resistance!

And these acts of day-to-day resistance are the factors that are making Ariel Sharon's plans to fail.

I would like to conclude by paying a tribute to the Israel small minority which is resisting too: the young **"Anarchists against the wall"**, who are there, on the wall, alone or together with Palestinians and with international activists, in order to protest, to disturb, to confront; the ladies of **Checkpoint Watch** standing every day on dozens of checkpoints in order to document the horrors of the closure, sometimes to intervene too; **women in Black,** standing in weekly vigils and confronting male hostility simply because they say "End the occupation!".

And a special tribute to the soldiers, reserve soldiers and young draftees, who are refusing to wear the occupation army uniform, and are sent to jail for their refusal. They are the true "Israeli heroes", the real allies of the Palestinian resistance, and the only bridge for an eventual future of peaceful coexistence between our peoples, based on equality, mutual respect and cooperation.

Palestine: Resistance to Liberation

Imam Achmad Cassiem

Islamic Unity Convention, South Africa

Abtsract

The author overviews attempts by US administrations to counter the effects of Liberation Theology in South America, citing specifically the setting up of the Institute of Religion & Democracy (IRD) and the production of the Santa Fe Document. The latter states that American foreign policy must begin to counterattack (and not just react against) Liberation Theology. Evidencing that these ideas, particularly those of theologians, can be subversive, this approach also characterises responses to faith based activism and resistance in Palestine. The author argues that the Palestinian problem centres on the concept of faith, and as such, therefore all perspectives, proposed solutions, objectives and goals must be defined within the parameters of this concept.

Based on the conceptual framework of the Qur'an, Palestine is entrusted to the Muslims. This trust (amanah) defines Muslim rights, obligations, methods and objectives in relation to Palestine. The primary objective of trustees is to serve the interest of Mankind, not of a particular socio-economic class, race, tribe or nation.

Resistance constitutes a law of nature and Islam endorses the natural law of resistance. However resistance is not sufficient to end or eradicate oppression.
Oppression and exploitation is upheld and entrenched by various forms of violence, including: structural violence; institutionalised violence; criminal violence; and revolutionary violence. Resistance can take various forms from: tactical resistance; strategic resistance; emotional resistance; intellectual resistance; moral resistance; spiritual resistance; and physical resistance.

Theologians do not provide a rationale to kill. To the extent that death is theologised it remains within the tradition of martyrdom reflecting the willingness to give one's life for others, not to take others lives. 'Ordinary people' usually turn to violence as a last resort for the purpose of self-defence, whereas oppressors resort to violence is usually the first option for the purposes of intimidation, aggression and terrorism. Oppressors negotiate when they stand to lose all, hence while Boycotts play a role in resistance it only armed struggle that forces the oppressor to the negotiation table.

Participation in the process of liberation means to be committed to the oppressed, as per Quranic principles *"And why should ye not fight in the Cause of Allah and the oppressed" (Quran 4:75)*

Coming to a conceptual understanding of the framework of Islam, understanding the terms of rights and obligations; embarking upon an aggregated and systematic analysis of our problems means that those concerned with liberation can plan an operational strategy for the creation and establishing of a new social order.

"Certainty (absolute conviction of the Truth) is the whole of Faith (Eemaan)" *(Hadith)*

"A.L.M. This is the Book; in it is guidance, sure, without doubt, to those who fear Allah; Who believe in the Unseen, are steadfast in prayer, and spend out of what We have provided for them; and who believe in the Revelation sent to thee, and sent before thy time, and (in their hearts) have the assurance of the Hereafter. They are on true guidance, from their Lord, and it is these who will prosper." (Qur'an 2:1-5)

Because of the political implications of a liberating Christianity, governments in various parts of the world have felt the need to take up positions either for or against liberation theology.

Alarm bells have rung most loudly in the United States. In 1969, President Nixon sent Nelson Rockefeller to Latin America to investigate the situation. His report stated that the church there was changing into "a force devoted to change, by revolutionary means in necessary".

The Report of the Rand Corporation, made at the request of the State Department in 1972, came to the same conclusion. Better known is the Santa Fé Document produced by advisors to President Reagan in 1982, which explicitly states: "American foreign policy must begin to counterattack (and not just react against) liberation theology".

In order to put this into effect, the Institute for Religion and Democracy (IRD) was set up in the United States, with the aim (amongst others) of mounting an ideological campaign against Latin American liberation theology.

A Catholic theologian at this Institute has stated: "Events in Iran and Nicaragua began to show political analysts that it is dangerous, when making their calculations, to omit the religious factor, particularly the ideas of theologians". [*Introducing Liberation Theology by Leonardo & Glodoris Boff – page 86; Burns & Gates 1987 – Britain*]

There can be no doubt that ideas, particularly the ideas of theologians, can be subversive; and that religion, once considered to be the opium of the people, needs to be taken more seriously.

As soon as the oppressed masses began to take religion seriously, the oppressors treated it with more respect. Is this a recurring historical phenomenon? If so, why?

Religion has been, and is being studied, from various perspectives. Sociology of religion is the scientific study of the behaviour of groups who are influenced by religious beliefs: Psychology of Religion is the scientific analysis of religious experiences and relating it to the rest of psychology: Philosophy of religion is the logical study of religious language and ideas: Theology is defined as the science which studies the facts and phenomena of religion and the relations between God and man. A distinction is drawn between natural theology and revealed theology. Theology is also seen as the attempt to talk rationally about the Divine – and therefore an explicit, systematic attempt to postulate doctrines in the light of faith.

Atheism, on the other hand, rejects Theism as an illusion, and theology as nonsense. It is interesting to note that the American State Department is so obsessed with this illusion and the nonsense articulated by theologians.

All religions manifest a theology, implicitly or explicitly. What is the relationship between theology and ideology?

We can have ideology minus theology; but we cannot have theology minus ideology (that is a rational set of principles, values and ideals.

Qur'anic Paradigm vs Theology

> "Say: 'What! Will you instruct Allah about your Religion? But Allah knows all that is in the Heavens and on Earth. He has full knowledge of all things." [Qur'an 49:16)

Islam is not a religion amongst other religions; Islam is **the** definition of religion. The Qur'an states the origin of religion as well as the purpose of religion. The Qur'an moves us out of the realm of theories into the realm of revelation. Theories are human constructs; they may be a summary of the state of our knowledge at a particular time but they can simultaneously be a summary of our ignorance at a particular point in time.

Theories undergo changes, modifications, amendments or are replaced by totally new ones! Revelation does not change – it is our understanding of it that changes, this understanding does not constitute a theory.

> "O ye who believe! Obey Allah and obey the Apostle, and those charged with authority amongst you. If ye differ in anything amongst yourselves, refer it to Allah and the Apostle, if you do believe in Allah and the Last Day: that is best and most suitable for final determination" (Qur'an 4:59)

The Qur'anic Paradigm frees us from theological speculation. The same is true of historical, scientific, and philosophical speculation.

The most serious intellectual challenge for those who deny the reality, truthfulness and validity of revelation, is to explain the 'Islamization of the Arabic language' beginning with the revelation of the Qur'an.

Rasulullah (SAWS) did not come to teach the Arabs Arabic; he came to teach them a new conceptual framework through the Arabic language.

Palestine in the Qur'anic Paradigm

"There is an excellent example (to follow) in Abraham and those with him, when they said to their people: 'We are clear of you and whatever you worship besides Allah the Almighty. We have you. There has arisen between us an everlasting animosity and hatred unless you believe in Allah the Almighty, and Him alone." (Qur'an 60:4)

In his book 'Palestine: Between Divine Law and Religion', Adnan Ali Rida al Nahwi maintains that this should be the real issue in the Palestinian problem. The problem centres on the concept of faith. All viewpoints, all perspectives regarding Palestine must begin with this concept. All proposed solutions, objectives and goals must be defined within the parameters of this concept. The Prophet Abraham migrated to Palestine because of faith.

"And this was the legacy that Abraham left to his sons, and so did Jacob: 'O my sons! Allah has chosen the faith for you; then die not except in the faith of Islam". (Qur'an 2:132)

The author states that the migration of the Prophet Abraham extended beyond Palestine to Makkah, where his wife Hajar gave birth to Ismail. This linked Palestine and the Hijaz.

"O Lord! Make us of Muslims, bowing to Thy (Will) and of our progeny a people Muslim, bowing to Thy (Will); and Show us the places for the celebration of due rites; and turn unto us (in Mercy); for Thy art the Oft-Returning, Most Merciful.

Our Lord! Send amongst them an Apostle of their own who shall rehearse Thy signs to them, instruct them in scripture and wisdom, and sanctify them for Thou art the Exalted in Might, Wise.

And who turns away from the religion of Abraham but such as destroy their souls with folly? Him we chose and rendered pure in this world; he will be in the Hereafter in the ranks of the Righteous. Behold! His Lord said to him: 'Bow (thy will) to Me': He said: 'I bow (my will) to the Lord and Cherisher of the Universe.'" (Qur'an 2:128-131)

The author maintains that all the Prophets (Abraham, Ismail, Isaac and Jacob) affirmed the right of Islam in Palestine (Qur'an 2:132 – 133). It is, therefore, one religion, one Prophethood, and one Ummah that possesses the true right of ownership of Palestine – the land as well as its legacy.

> "Abraham was not a Jew, nor a Christian; but he was true in Faith, and bowed his will to Allah (which is Islam, and he joined not gods with God." (Qur'an 3:67)

Faith is based on the conceptual framework derived from Qur'an. Moses also led the people out of slavery to Palestine to continue the Message of Faith.

> "O my people! Enter the Holy Land which Allah hath assigned to you, and turn not back ignominiously, for then will ye be overthrown to your ruin." (Qur'an 10:83-84)

The author correctly contends that Palestine was therefore holy land before Moses entered it. He was followed by Yuoh'a bin Neron, David and Soloman. There was no racism, no nationalism; all were Muslim. This is the legacy of Prophethood extending throughout history.

> "It was We who revealed the law (to Moses); therein was guidance and light …If any fail to judge by (the light of) what God hath revealed, they are (no better than) Unbelievers." (Qur'an 5:47)

Jesus too was sent to restore the true Message of Faith.

> "And remember Jesus, the son of Mary, said: 'O Children of Israel! I am the Apostle of Allah (sent) to you, confirming the Law (which came) before me, and giving glad tidings of an Apostle to come after me, whose name shall be Ahmad." (Qur'an 61:6)

The Night Journey (from Makkah to Jerusalem) of the Prophet Muhammad (SAWS) was another assurance of the rights of Islam in Palestine: the NEXUS OF FAITH and the NEXUS OF POWER were confirmed.

One single Ummah possesses the right to own Palestine and to defend it against its enemies. Palestine is a trust in the hands of Muslims based on the conceptual framework of the Qur'an. This trust (amánah) defines our rights, obligations, methods and objectives with regards to Palestine. The primary objective is to serve the interests of mankind – not that of a particular socio-economic class, race, tribe or nation.

Palestine is the responsibility of each and every Muslim on the face of the Earth. Palestine is an integral part of the Divine Call of Islam.

> "Thus have we made of you an Ummah justly balanced, that you might be

witnesses over the nations, and the Prophet a witness over yourselves: and we appointed the Qibla to which thou was used, only to test those who would turn on their heels (from the Faith)."

The Nature of Resistance

Resistance is a law of Nature. Islam being the natural way of life endorses this natural law of resistance.

Before resistance sets in, there is only the prospect of subjection, capitulation and defeat. Therefore we must ask the following questions:

(i)   Resist What?
(ii)   Resist Whom?
(iii)   Why Resist?
(iv)   When to Resist?
(v)   Where to Resist?
(vi)   How to Resist?

Once we have answered these questions we are in a position to respond to:

a) What is the PURPOSE of resistance?
b) What is the OBJECTIVE of resistance?

We will realise soon enough that Resistance is not sufficient to
(i)   Stop oppression
(ii)   End oppression
(iii)   Eradicate oppression

Violence

In the final analysis all types of oppression and exploitation are upheld and entrenched by various forms of violence.

1) Structural Violence – built into the infrastructure and superstructure of the social order. We cannot say that the people have a right to life and then deny them the RIGHT TO THE MEANS TO SUSTAIN THAT LIFE.
2) Institutionalized violence – organs of state or special organs of government use violence
3) Criminal and anti-social violence – organized crime disorganizes the social order.
4) Revolutionary Violence

Types of Resistance

A. TACTICAL RESISTANCE: Day to day resistance to occupy the enemy; to raise the morale of the masses.

B. STRATEGIC RESISTANCE: Resistance which forms part of a broader plan to destroy and eliminate the system of oppression. Pre-emptive resistance is a major facet of strategic resistance.

Dimensions of Resistance

1. Emotional Resistance – anger, hatred
2. Intellectual Resistance – fight ideas with better ideas; when there is a paradigm shift, the enemy is at position zero. Very important for morale.
3. Moral Resistance – morale means not only fighting spirit but more importantly the <u>morality</u> of the people who have this fighting spirit
4. Spiritual Resistance – sincerity, purpose, intention, and integrity of resistance upheld.
5. Physical Resistance – inclusive of armed resistance.

Beyond Resistance – Liberation

Whereas Christian Liberation Theology is described as:

(1) An interpretation of Christian faith out of the suffering, struggle and hope of the poor;
(2) A theological critique of society and its ideological underpinnings;
(3) A critique of the practice of the Church of the Christians

(*Introduction to Liberation Theology by Phillip Berryman*)

It would be absurd to postulate an "Islamic Liberation Theology" for the Qur'anic Paradigm cannot be reduced to a mere interpretation or a critique. The Qur'anic paradigm is precise and definitive, and is therefore liberation from theological speculation.

On page 195 of Berryman's book he says:

> "Ratzinger (Cardinal, now Pope Benedict) echoes others who, perhaps with priest-guerillas in mind, believe liberation theology seeks to provide a rationale for revolutionary violence. In fact no theologian has written a book on the issue. No theologian has provided a theological rationale for killing. To the extent that death is theologized, it is in reflections on martyrdom, the willingness to give one's life for others, not to take others' lives."

Berryman continues:

"When ordinary people turn to violence, it is generally a last resort and in their minds is essentially self-defence. In any case, it does not derive from liberation theology."

We comment that when oppressors resort to violence, it is normally as the first option – and is not considered self-defence but intimidation, aggression and terrorism.

In any case, any "theology" that does not deal with matters of life and death (self-defence etc) is inadequate and impotent.

The Qur'anic Paradigm for Liberation

The Qur'an affirms and confirms the unity of the human family and its common origin; it also postulates the innate dignity of human beings. Poverty is a consequence of oppression – it is the cause which must be tackled and not merely the symptoms.

> "And why should ye not fight in the Cause of Allah and the oppressed (Mustadafin)" (Qur'an 4:75)

Participation in the process of liberation means to be committed to the oppressed.

> *"O Allah let me live amongst the poor, let me die amongst the poor, and on the Day of Resurrection raise me up amongst the poor."* (Hadith)

To know the real world of oppression and exploitation is part of the religious school of thought.

The Qur'anic Paradigm negates theological speculation; that is why Muslims are not entrapped in Black theology, Hispanic theology and Feminist theology.

There has to be

(1) Unity of Thought
(2) Unity of Purpose
(3) Unity of Expression
(4) Unity in Action

And we can arrive at this goal by stressing and focusing on

i)   Conceptual literacy – understanding the conceptual framework of Islam correctly; then be socialized in terms of rights and obligations

ii)   Embarking upon a systems' analysis of our problem areas instead of just a components analysis

iii)   Planning an operational strategy for the creation and establishing of a new social order!

"There is no Islam without social cohesion, social interaction, social commitment"

The Right of Resistance:
A Christian Palestinian Perspective

Rev Stephen Sizer

Friends of Sabeel , UK

Abtsract

Presenting the work of Sabeel, the Palestinian Liberation Theology Centre, based in Jerusalem, the author looks at non-violent approaches to the occupation, focussing on morally responsible investment. He looks at the biblical grounds for opposing evil and contextualises resistance within the Christian discourse of God's love, justice, mercy and peace. He closes with extracts from a letter from Sabeel's Naim Ateek, asking how Christmas can be celebrated when such suffering is taking place in Palestine.

In this short paper I want to present to you a Christian perspective on the right of resistance, within the context of the Palestinian struggle. I want to speak on behalf of Sabeel. They have just produced a new document called *"A Non-violent Approach to the Occupation: A call for morally responsible investment"*. (Sabeel, Jerusalem, 2005). I would like to present selected parts in this presentation. As an ecumenical Christian organisation committed to both interfaith dialogue and non-violence, Sabeel emphasizes the importance of faithfulness to God – the God of love, justice, mercy, and peace.

The Bible teaches us that all people are created in God's image and are loved equally and unconditionally. We also believe that the creator, God, has sanctified humanity through the Incarnation of Jesus Christ. The dignity of every human being is precious in the eyes of God. Jesus said, *"I have come in order that you might have life – life in all its fullness"* (John 10:10). For people to enjoy life in its fullness, they must live in peace and justice, in dignity and harmony with each other. Their God-given human worth must be respected. We must do everything we can to remove any obstacles that prevent human beings from the possibility of achieving life in its fullness. What are the Biblical grounds for resistance against evil?

1. Our Mandate is Justice and Mercy

"He has told you, O mortal, what is good; and what does the Lord require of you but to do justice, and to love mercy, and to walk humbly with your God? (Micah 6:8).

"Love your neighbour as yourself" (Mark 12:31)

2. Our Means are Scripture & Truth (prophetic non-violence)

"Put on the full armour of God so that you can take your stand against the devil's schemes... Take the helmet of salvation and the sword of the Spirit, which is the word of God." (Ephesians 6:11, 17)

"Jesus said, "My kingdom is not of this world. If it were, my servants would fight to prevent my arrest by the Jews. But now my kingdom is from another place." "You are a king, then!" said Pilate. Jesus answered, "You are right in saying I am a king. In fact, for this reason I was born, and for this I came into the world, to testify to the truth. Everyone on the side of truth listens to me..." (John 18:36-37)

3. Our Motive is Peace and Reconciliation

"Blessed are the peacemakers, for they will be called children of God." (Matthew 5:9).

"All this is from God, who reconciled us to himself through Christ and gave us the ministry of reconciliation: that God was reconciling the world to himself in Christ, not counting men's sins against them. And he has committed to us the message of reconciliation." (2 Corinthians 5:18-19)

[This is our right - indeed our mandate, our imperative - as Christ followers - to resist oppression, to challenge those who seek to thwart or destroy God's laws for human society - to do justice, and love mercy, and walk humbly with God].

We also believe that the best embodiments of such laws as they apply in the international arena are enshrined in the Universal Declaration of Human Rights and International Humanitarian Law, which includes the Fourth Geneva Convention, as well as other universally accepted principles of international law protecting human rights and human dignity.

There are multiple examples of violations of human rights in Palestine. International humanitarian law specifies that people living under occupation (like the Palestinians on the West Bank, Gaza Strip and East Jerusalem) must be protected until the occupation comes to an end. It is illegal to build on or confiscate their land.

It is illegal to harm innocent civilians. It is forbidden to employ collective punishment, degrading treatment and torture.
It is illegal to transfer parts of an occupying powers' civilian population into occupied territories. International law also forbids the acquisition of territory through war. From the standpoint of faith, we believe that we must recognize and name the evils that are facing the peoples of Israel-Palestine on both sides of the conflict. We must act responsibly under God. God calls us to value all people and stand up for all who are suffering and oppressed.

Jesus specifically rebuked those who exploited or abused the poor. "They devour widows' houses and for a show make lengthy prayers. Such men will be punished most severely." (Mark 12:40) This is why James, the brother of Jesus, challenges and rebukes those who oppress the poor.

> "The wages you failed to pay the workmen who mowed your fields are crying out against you. The cries of the harvesters have reached the ears of the Lord Almighty. You have lived on earth in luxury and self-indulgence. You have fattened yourselves in the day of slaughter. You have condemned and murdered innocent men, who were not opposing you." (James 5:4-6)

Wealth is power. And power invariably leads to exploitation which creates more wealth for the powerful. The contrast between rich and poor in 1st Century Palestine was not that dissimilar to the contrasts between the settlements and refugee camps of Palestine today. It is just that the occupying powers are different. So the warning of Jesus and his apostles must be spoken prophetically today.

James summarises what authentic faith looks like.

> "Religion that God our Father accepts as pure and faultless is this: to look after orphans and widows in their distress and to keep oneself from being polluted by the world." (James 1:27)

Such a stand leads us [for example] to responsible stewardship in the investments we make as individuals, churches and institutions. As Christians we [repudiate] those who carry out unethical, immoral, and illegal actions. We have a God-given responsibility to act. We cannot ourselves participate even indirectly in supporting and enabling unjust policies.

In this context, therefore, we need to contemplate the following:
1. Earning money through investment in companies whose products and services are used in such a way as to violate international law and human rights is equivalent to profiting from unlawful acts and from the oppression of others.
2. Investment in such companies can be seen as condoning the harm of innocent civilians under occupation and the illegal Israeli settlement policies that lead to human rights violations.
3. Investment in such companies enables the government of Israel to sustain the ongoing violation of human rights of innocent civilians.
4. Continuing such investments once the facts are brought to our attention constitutes deliberate condoning of the evil practices.

"Our goal is to promote Israel's compliance with international humanitarian law. Divestment is a means to enact our obligation to prevent any assistance or participation in the violations of these basic human rights [because] we have an ethical duty to prevent unlawful harm to civilians. It is clearly demonstrated that Israel, in its continued occupation and the practices associated with the occupation, is in open violation of international law and specifically the provisions of the Fourth Geneva Convention. Violations of these articles, specifically the grave breaches (Art. 147) have been defined as war crimes."

How Do We Aassist Israel to Escape from its Illegal and Immoral Status?

A system of international economic support for the occupation today exists as multinational corporations build franchises in the occupied territories, supply military goods, and provide material for the construction of the separation wall. Although numerous U.N. resolutions have been passed and many countries have pleaded with Israel to change its policies, the "facts on the ground" of occupation grow worse year by year. The goal to end the occupation has never seemed farther.

At this point in time, then, assessing the international community's efforts to persuade Israel through the United Nations and the International High Court to have had little effect, we look at other options. Around the world, people are beginning to speak of selective divestment from Israel as a method to create the change that is needed. As responsible owners, the churches as investors have multiple economic options. The dictionary defines divestment as "to free of," "to sell off," "to dispossess". Today, there are many methods of investment and divestment including these five strategies:

1. **Avoidance strategy**, i.e. avoiding investment in companies on moral grounds.
2. **Involvement strategy**, i.e. exercising influence in shareholder meetings to actively promote corporate social responsibility.
3. **Alternative strategy or selective investment**, i.e. establishing alternative investment funds that promote justice and peace.
4. **Withdrawal strategy**, i.e. simply pulling investments on moral grounds.
5. **Reinvestment strategy**, i.e. moving the money from investments on moral grounds but being certain to reinvest it in similar organizations that work for positive change.

What methods do Sabeel recommend? We agree that selective divestment; a model that has been advocated by the World Council of Churches, the Presbyterian Church USA as well as many organizations working for a just peace in the region is the next logical step. Therefore, Sabeel [is calling on] churches to divest from corporations that:
1. provide products, services or technology that sustain, support or maintain the occupation;
2. have established facilities or operations on occupied land;
3. provide products, services, or financial support for the establishment, expansion, or maintenance of settlements on occupied land or settlement related infrastructure;

4. provide products, services or financial backing to groups that commit violence against innocent civilians; and
5. provide finance or assist in the construction of Israel's separation wall or settlement infrastructure.

Sabeel believes that any divestment must be done from moral obligation – the same moral obligation that obliges us to struggle against and separate ourselves from anti-Semitism. From a Christian perspective, we have a right and moral obligation to resist oppression while still loving even our enemies.

We are reminded of the words of the South American liberation theologian, Leonardo Boff:

"If we want to serve the true God, we must break out of the circle of self-absorption and pay heed to the bloodied faces of our fellow human beings. If we do not share life with the oppressed, we do not share life with God." (Leonardo Boff)

I would like to close with a prayer,

"May the Justice of God fall down like fire and bring a home for the Palestinian. May the mercy of God fall down like rain and protect the Jewish people. And may the holy eyes of a beautiful God, who weeps for all his children, bring his healing hope to his wounded ones to the Jew and the Palestinian." Garth Hewitt

I want to end by reading to you part of the letter sent by Naim Ateek, founder and director of Sabeel, last Christmas. It is called "The Defiant Spirit of Christmas", and reflects the right of resistance, which Palestinian Christians feel.
Naim asks, how is it possible to celebrate [as Christians] with all the closures and checkpoints, with all the injustice and oppression, with all the violations of human rights, with the presence of a wall that separates families and friends, and a multitude of hardships that the occupation imposes to make people's lives miserable, how can we speak of love, peace and joy when most of our people and millions of others around the world do not experience liberty and peace?

The questions are legitimate. Yet as peace-makers, following in the footsteps of the Prince of Peace, Christians are called to the path of non-violent resistance in hope and anticipation, with determination and zeal to work for a better world where people can experience these essential qualities of life.

Therefore, wherever empire exists and the powers that be are in control through domination, there is a greater responsibility for all of us to take a stand against all that dehumanizes people and to work for their liberation. "The Christmas story is a story of a liberating God who comes to join an oppressed people in the work of liberation. God's message through the angels is a message of defiance. In spite of the presence of empire, human arrogance, and oppression, God is announcing peace and goodwill.

This is God's agenda. Glory belongs to God and not to the emperor nor to the powers. Once that is genuinely acknowledged, peace is not far away. It is in the midst of the Roman occupation that the Incarnation took place; it is in spite of the occupation that Mary and Joseph found joy and love in the birth of Jesus; it is in spite of the occupation and in the midst of economic hardships that the shepherds came to visit a family of modest means and discovered great joy and peace; it is in spite of the occupation that the Magi came to offer their gifts to the child. We celebrate in the midst of the occupation and in spite of it. Through our celebration we defy the occupation; we defy the injustice; we defy the oppressors; we defy the powers. They do not possess the last word, they can build high walls, but they cannot take away our hope, they can put us in jail, but they cannot take away our joy, they can prevent us from visiting family, but they cannot take away our love, they can stop us at checkpoints and impose all kinds of restrictions, but they cannot take away our pursuit of freedom and liberation, they can prevent us from going to Bethlehem, but they cannot prevent the spirit of Bethlehem from reaching us, they can treat us as nonhumans, but they cannot crush our spirit nor can they take away our God-given human worth and dignity, they can act with hate and disgust but, by the grace of God, we can always refuse to stoop to the level of hate and maintain our love of God and neighbour that includes them. Therefore Christmas makes us defiant. We defy the evildoers because we believe in the goodness of which they are capable of doing, we defy hate because we believe in the power of love and forgiveness, we defy despair because we believe in life and hope, we defy violence and terror - both state and individual - because we believe in the power of peace and non-violence, we defy war and the occupation of other people's lands because we believe in the power of peaceful methods based on international law and legitimacy, we defy and challenge those who humiliate and degrade others because we believe in the dignity of every human being. The Incarnation took place when God took on our humanity, when the Word became flesh and dwelt among us. This happened in Palestine under Roman occupation. Then as now and in spite of all the hardships, we celebrate Christ's birth, Emmanuel, God with us, giving us hope, joy, peace, and love. We are defiant. We are full of hope. We will continue to work for peace through justice. Glory to God in the Highest and on Earth Peace." Naim Ateek

The Dismantling of Israel via an Islamic Theology of Justice and Liberation

Imam Muhammad Al-Asi

Institute of Contemporary Islamic Thought, Washington DC, USA

Abstract

The war on terror has been used by the US as a means to justify the steady erosion of rights and freedoms of the American people as witness through the Patriot Act, the admission of secret evidence into courts, the profiling of suspect. These measures are justified on the basis of "National Security"; the logic implies that national rights take precedence over individual rights.

But if the erosion of individual rights is justified on the basis of persevering the larger society, it begins to discriminate and segregate that individual, his ethnicity race or religion from the larger society. This has a serious corroding influence on the fabric of a multi-ethnic, trans-racial and equal opportunity driven society.

Moreover, the violation of an individual and/or ethnic minority's right in one country set a dangerous precedence, potentially leading to even greater reactionary consequences in another country. The absence of God as a legitimising concept in all human socio-political arrangements has created an increasingly volatile and violent world.

Palestine, the Holy Land or Israel presents one the most intractable problem of human history. Firstly the problem presented is the exclusive claims of two separate peoples to one common land. Secondly is the asymmetry between the unparalleled military might on the side of the Zionists and the undiminished will to fight on the side of the Palestinians. Thirdly is the hyped up but false Judaization on the Israeli side and the systematic de-Islamization on the side of the Palestinian (although in recent years the latter trend has been in slow reverse). The author argues for a new approach to rediscover the religious component of the Palestinian issue.

Justice and equity are central concepts to be found in the scripture of all three of the monotheistic faith tradition. The corresponding lack of these concepts in public discourse is contributing to, not solving the issue of Palestine. The genesis of liberation theology gives justification for the combination of people and land on the basis of justice and equity. The absence of justice fortifies the group rights to the holy land regardless of religious claims.

Human relations and human rights are a complex web of issues if we are to go by the current political and economic requirements of today's world order. One particular cornerstone of today's international standards is **The Universal Declaration of Human Rights** which is a charter of civil and political rights drawn up by the United Nations in 1948. They include the right to life, liberty, education, and equality before the law; to freedom of movement, religion, association, and information; and to a nationality. Under the European Convention of Human Rights (1950), the Council of Europe established the **European Commission of Human Rights** (headquarters in Strasbourg, France), which investigates complaints by states or individuals, and its findings are examined by the **European Court of Human Rights** (established 1959), whose compulsory jurisdiction has been recognized by a number of states, including the United Kingdom (UK). And as far as the nation-state system in Europe and North America is concerned these legalisms and legalities seem to be in a state of homeostasis. Outside this geopolitical area the world is in an uneasy and potentially volatile state of existence. The general "state of the world" is tense, seemingly irreconcilable, and characterized by military flare-ups from generation to generation and from country to country. We, who live in Euro-American societies and "enjoy" the fruits of "modernity", have been exposed to an "education" about the rights and freedoms of society. This can be traced to post-renaissance Europe and its accompanying political philosophies. The American war of "independence" also ushered in theoretical and liberal ideas about freedom and liberty as well as the French Revolution in the last thirty years of the 18th century.

Nowadays human rights are the catchwords in our post-modern politics and social discourse. The theoretical flowery discourse on human rights and freedoms is one thing and the practice is sometimes altogether another thing. Authoritarians and totalitarians have discovered that human freedoms and rights become a "threat" or a diminishment of their excessive and concentrated power. There can never be a legitimate and permanent valid argument for the violation or the alteration of inalienable human rights. But autocratic and monarchic establishments will try to rationalize their anti-human rights position with whatever is at their disposal.

One of the public relations arguments for the curtailment of God-given human freedoms inalienable human rights is that national rights are a priority over individual rights. This is often used to justify a particular state's military budget and military strategy when in a state of war with another state. A similar argument now is taking shape in the United States as the government proceeds to justify its international war against terrorism by diminishing the rights and freedoms of its own citizens. Witness the Patriot Act and the rolling back of certain liberties and freedoms: the admission of secret evidence into courts of law, security agencies profiling of "suspect" individuals at airports, and a host of other procedures and acts that in the absence of a "national security threat" would be unthinkable. The general argument here is that for the security of the American people some American individuals will have to forego their privacy rights, their civic rights, the human rights, and their legal rights.

This may seem, on the surface of it, quite acceptable. After all, there will be no individual freedom if the citizenry that individual belongs to is threatened and potentially ruined. But if the erosion of individual rights is justified on the basis of preserving the larger society it begins to discriminate and segregate that individual and his ethnicity or race or religion from the larger society it belongs to. This is a serious wearing away at the multi-ethnic and trans-racial and equal opportunity society that belongs to everyone regardless of their individuality. Besides, the world itself is shrinking into a global village and peoples are dispersed into a more strongly felt international society. And the violation of an "individual's" or an "ethnic" minority's human rights in one country can have equal if not more reactionary consequences on others in another country.

The other argument for human "inequality" is to say that not everyone should enjoy the equal position in a particular legal system because some people are not as equal as others. This argument is concentrated in racist communities and states. Sometimes this argument confuses equality with uniformity. It is true that people are not homogenized and harmonious in cultural ways. But this does not give a political system and an established government the right to treat its subjects unequally in a society's market of opportunities or in a government's court of law.

Another corrosive effect on human rights is their interpretation in a way that causes some classes or segments of society to enjoy certain rights when those same rights feed on the depravation or the discrimination allotted to the "other."

***

The overall pool of social norms and laws that have come to dominate our world are, by and large, secular. Human rights in the contemporaneous world, although they sound reasonable and practical, have not had a very positive impact on global society and have not deterred civil wars, regional wars, and world wars. The underlying reason for this undesirable and increasingly volatile human strain is the absence of God's concepts and codes in the arrangement of social issues, affairs, and events.

As far as this paper goes, I will concentrate on some of the major issues that have converged to give us one of the most intractable problems in human history: Palestine, the Holy Land, or Israel.

The first anomaly that feeds this problem is the exclusive claim of two separate peoples to one common land. The second snarl and snag is the symmetry between the unparallel military might of one side (the Zionists) and the undiminished will to fight on the other (the Palestinians). And the third conundrum is a hyped up (but false) Judaization of the Israeli side of this problem throughout the past years which corresponds to a systemic de-Islamization of the Palestinian side of this problem since 1947; with this trend being in slow reverse as of recent years.

The "Christian" component of this complex polarization has been roughly split into the "Christians" with an Islamic culture who have been "lumped" with the Palestinians, and the "Christians" with a "Euro-American" political affinity who have been either passively or actively on the "Israeli" side of this clash. For purposes of brevity, we shall steer clear of the "Christian" component of this historical and contemporary encounter with its ideological and military expressions.

***

Our approach here is to rediscover the "religious" component of the Palestinian issue without, as much as possible, becoming drawn into the fossilized presentation of this two-sided Judeo-Islamic controversy.

It is our understanding that God centered His Scriptures and Revelations on the issue of justice. Justice has always been foremost, central, and enduring in the lives of Old Testament, New Testament, and Qur'anic prophets and apostles (i).

This presence of the meaning of justice and equity in Scripture and its lack from public discourse (political, social, economic, religious, etc...) is contributing to, not solving, the issue of Palestine.

If the Jews and the Muslims could come to a common concentration on the cardinal issue of justice they will begin to discover that work has to be done to alleviate the injustice that has been simmering in and around the Holy Land. Along these lines the two religious communities [Jews and Muslims] will have to address the issue of belonging to the Holy Land. And they will discover that what is called Palestine (in the geographical and historical usage of the word) is a land of the powerful meant for a people without power, or a land without justice meant for a people with justice. The historical formula has always been that powerless people will bring God's justice to that land.

This becomes the genesis of the Liberation Theology that gives justification for the combination of people and land on the basis of justice and equality. Any failure to stand for and live up to the principles of justice and equity forfeits the right of any political orientation of people regardless of their religious professions to the Holy Land.

The Islamic approach to this issue takes into consideration the fundamental issue of justice which knows no discrimination on the basis of religion, ethnicity, race, or "social" class. Mature Muslims who have de-fossilized their Islam are keenly aware of the relationship between belonging to God's Covenant and belonging to His land. As much as the secular world would like to ignore or obfuscate this issue, the fact of the matter is that countries are run by civic societies or national blocs of people, with justice being a function or a feature of that nationality, and with lesser justice or no justice to others who are not thoroughly or "exclusively" of that particular nationality (ii).

It transpires from this reading of history with justice as its key component that the land of Palestine is meant for powerless people who are worried about and possessed with justice. In the course of history there were prophet clustered people who were given the responsibility of carrying out justice after having to fight to prove their qualities and their dedication. The Mosaic congregation [pertaining to Moses (P)] at one time failed this power-test for justice (iii). No amount of self-piety or religious symbolism was going to substitute for their abandoning the cause of justice.

The Roman occupation of that same land could be viewed from the same perspective. It was the mission of Jesus (P) to reinvigorate man's relationship with God to eventually accumulate with a keen sense of justice that will in time bring down the power-structure that hides behind a facade of justice but in reality is the administrator of injustice there and in other places.

The "break-through" came with the advent of the justice-centred Muslims who left the Arabian Peninsula in the 7th century AD to finally sweep in an era of social, political, and economic justice that was inclusive of Jews, Christians, and Muslims. But as the centuries went by, the justice character of the "Muslims" themselves began to erode. This Muslim "justice failure" gave way to the "Crusades" and their century long occupation of that same land. In time, the Muslims regrouped, mustered their will-power, and refocused on the issue of justice; the result was to last until WWI when justice was no longer a crucial feature of Islamic governance.

The post-WWI world had entered into its new secular phase. Justice now was no longer a divine responsibility, a Scriptural requirement for social emancipation, or a legal standard with its "Jewish", "Christian," or "Islamic" origins. Colonialism and Imperialism had run amok in the Islamic hemisphere of the world. Countries were carved out of stochastic formulas; regions were torn apart through colonialist and imperialist rivalries. And in a matter of a couple of generations the Muslim populations had to endure a long night of mis-representative governments, governments having no popular support and no legitimacy. In this dark political era when Muslims the world over lost their "ummah" – their united homeland, the Zionists were traveling in the opposite direction, trying to regain their *Eretz Israel* via a movement of Jewish people undergoing their *alia*.

Centuries upon centuries of a particular diaspora propelled many Jews out of their sub-national ghettoes throughout Europe in particular to settle in what they dreamed of as the land of return. There was and there is no universal or Scriptural standard or justice that can define this movement of Jews who were tricked by Zionist propaganda into believing that a nationalist-cum-racist state of Israel will become their refuge and their native land. In the absence of the God-given principle and standard of justice the long awaited "Israel" turned out to be what it is today: a multi-national ghetto! Prime Minister Sharon is hemming in the fact by the seven hundred mile barrier that separates the Semitic peoples of the Holy Land! Zionism had become the convenient instrument that rode the tide of nationalism from Europe into Palestine. A Gentile European inflicted diaspora of Jews, henceforth created a diaspora of Semitic Palestinians, all in the name of a Zionism devoid of justice. Power became paramount and justice was junked. It is this theatre of injustice which began its final chapter in 1947 that begs for a solution. Preceding this final Zionist solution were the immediate and earlier increments that set the stage for a Holy Land without justice and the Zionist military occupation of Palestine. The issue that has to be emphasized here is the corrupt, one-sided, unjust, and nefarious nature of the Zionist Israeli governments from beginning to end. In 1869 the Jewish Colonization Association begins in Palestine.

Theodore Herzl iv, a journalist, publishes *Der Judenstaat*, advocating establishment of a Zionist state in Palestine or elsewhere. In 1901, pressured by triumphant European powers, the Ottoman government [at the end of almost a century of defensive wars against Europe, allows foreign Zionists to buy land in northern Palestine. In 1903 a second wave of Zionist mass immigration moves into Palestine. In 1917, the British Secretary of State Balfour (v) pledges British support of a "Jewish national home in Palestine" in the Balfour Declaration(vi). In 1923 resigning from the Zionist executive, Polish Zionist leader Vladimir Jabotinsky(vii) calls for the forcible colonization of Palestine and Transjordan. In 1946 the total Jewish population in Palestine reached 610,000. The population of Palestinian natives was 1.3 million. 93% of Palestinian land was owned by non-Jewish Palestinians. In 1948 the United Nations issues its Partition Plan – 56% of land designed for accommodation of a Jewish state while 43% was given to the native Palestinians. This resulted in the first all-out war between the two sides. The result: Israel usurps 75% of the land. In 1956, with Zionist Jews in a military ascending order and the non-representative governments in surrounding countries in a secular infliction the second "Arab-Israeli" war breaks out. Israel attacks Egypt after nationalization of the Suez Canal Company and later retreats.

In 1967 the Six Day War breaks out. Israel ends up occupying East Jerusalem and the West Bank, administered by Jordan, the Ghazzah Strip (administered by Egypt) and the Sinai peninsula, and Syria's Golan Heights.

In 1973 the fourth "Arab-Israeli" war erupts. Egypt and Syria both make spurious and limited military gains.

In 1987 the first intifadah (uprising) starts against Israeli occupation in the Ghazzah Strip, West Bank, and East Jerusalem.

In 2000 the second intifadah ignites. The death of a 12 year-old Palestinian boy, Muhammad al-Durrah, caught on camera as he is shot to death while hiding behind his shielding father shocks the world.

In 2002 the apartheid Israeli government begins building a skyline barrier throughout 10 of the 11 West Bank districts. This enclosure that impedes free movement annexes nearly 50% of the West Bank and completely destroys all continuity of life for the Palestinians in the region.

In 2005 the Israeli racial segregationist government continues its systemic policies of legal discrimination with its ongoing dispossession, displacement, and diaspora of the Semitic Palestinian people.

In this scenario of climaxing events the Israeli government represents the best tradition of power arrogance and hegemonistic hubris. The injustice and tyranny that have become synonymous with the word "Israel" may be encapsulated further by looking at the following facts:

In 1948 over 800,000 Palestinians are forced to leave their homes due to bellicose and belligerent Zionist attacks.

In 1967 another 300,000 Palestinians are made refugees by the "power-over-justice" Israeli government.

Since September 29, 2000: around 30,000 Palestinians have been injured, around 4,000 have been killed (700 of which were children), and around 4,500 Palestinian homes have been demolished.

Between March 2001 and July 11, 2003 more than 60 new Jewish-only settlements have been built on confiscated Palestinian land.

Today there are over four million (4,000,000) Palestinian refugees. Around 8,500 Palestinians are imprisoned by the intolerant anti-Semitic Israeli government.

If anything, the government in Tel Aviv has established its superior record in violation of all standards of fairness and all principles of justice.

Israel's treacherous and seditious policies extend to other parts of the world.

Honduras

"In 1981 Leo Gleser, "co-owner" of International Security and Defense Systems (ISDS) – a leading Israeli "security" firm identified repeatedly as an Israeli entity – began building Battalion 316, a unit of Honduran military intelligence which disappeared, tortured, then killed its victims."(viii)

South Africa

"1986-91. Israrel trained members of Inkatha hit squads aimed at the African National Congress, a disillusioned former leader of Zulu organization has revealed."(ix)

Guatemala

"1970-87. Violence by security forces organized by the CIA, trained in torte by advisors from Argentina and Chile and supported by weapon/computer experts from Israel."(x)

Mozambique

"Israel has also been involved with the Mozambican "contras." The South African-backed MNR (Mozambique National Resistance or "Renamo"), which has brought great economic and social distress to Mozambique."(xi)

Panama

"It was no surprise. Noriega had undergone military and intelligence training in Israel, jumped five times with Israeli paratroopers, and – like Uganda's deposed dictator Idi Amin – proudly wore his Israeli paratrooper wings on his uniform for many years afterwards. Although critics say America "bought and paid" for Noriega, he was also an Israeli creation and a great admirer of the ruthless Israeli way, as was Amin, the most brutal despot in 20th century African history(xii).

The Israeli Likud and Labor parties have never tired of perfecting their record of despotism and racism. The structured and systematic injustice has become legend. Testimonies about this come from multiple sources.

"Israel's policy of destruction of Palestinian homes, coupled with tight restrictions and discriminatory practices against Palestinians applying for building permits has resulted in losses of homes for over 16,700 Palestinians (including 7,300 children) since 1987."(xiii)

"Since 1967, Israel has confiscated an estimated 60% of the West Bank, 33% of the Ghazzah Strip and 33% of the Palestinian land in Jerusalem is for public, semi-public and private use in order to create Israeli military zones, settlements, industrial areas, elaborate 'bypass' roads, and quarries, as well as to hold 'State land' for exclusive Israeli use."(xiv)

"...around 70 percent of children in the Ghazzah Strip have been exposed to 4 or 5 traumatic events such as tear-gas inhalation, night raids on the home, humiliation and/or beating of parents in front of them by Israeli forces and imprisonment."(xv)

"...furthermore, during the past ten years 46,000 kids under the age of 18 have become disabled due to the use of live ammunition and metal coated rubber bullets by the Israeli army. An additional 34,000 adults over the age of 18 have also become disabled by the Israeli army."(xvi)

"Israel's methods of extracting information from detainees include abuses such as position abuse, hooding, prolonged sleep deprivation, exposure to immensely loud music, violent shaking, threats, and chilling by cold air which are in breach of the Convention against Torture."(xvii)

And if further testimony is needed for the travesty of justice called Israel, the following statements come from the "horse's mouth".

"I don't know something called international principles. I vow that I'll burn every Palestinian child [that] will be born in this area."(xviii)

"There is no such thing as a Palestinian people... It is not as if we came and threw them out and took their country. They didn't exist."(xix)

"What you don't understand is that the dirty work of Zionism is not finished yet, far from it."(xx)
"In a report released earlier this week by the B'tselem Human Rights Organization, the term 'rubber bullets' used by Israeli forces is misleading, explaining that the rubber-coated metallic bullets are deadly despite their name."(xxi)

***

Islam: The Only Decisive Solution

There have been and continue to be a stream of statements about political or radical Islam; some of them coming from friends others coming from foes. Not many of them though are able to formulate a strategic and all-inclusive response to the challenge of Zionism and Israel. We hope that the non-exhaustive facts above give a clear picture of the violent, ruthless, and expansionist nature of Zionism and Israel, because that is necessary to understand the Islamic revolutionary and theological answer to the Zionist occupation of a people's country and the Zionist oppression of a country's population. If we could neutralize all highbrow and pejorative projections of "Islamic Fundamentalism" for a moment and begin with fresh statements we would put it this way.

Islam is a theological ideology and an ideological theology compressed into one Scripture. Its primary and principal concern is with justice.(xxii) Injustice is anathema to dedicated and devout Muslims (xxiii) . The historical covenant of God's relationship with people is not defined by a people's race but rather by people's convictions and principles (xxiv) . And these convictions and principles are rooted in social justice, equity, and equality.(xxv) Therefore, this lifelong struggle for justice against injustice becomes the "religious" character of sincere and wholehearted Muslims.

For Muslims the nation-state of Israel is evil, without any second question or doubt. The fact that Israel is capable of camouflaging its nature by hiding behind a system of nation states around it has not been thoroughly developed in the contemporary Islamic liberation discourse. The fact that has still to dawn on many Islamic activists is that the majority of Muslim peoples have been enthralled to a nation-state system in the Islamic East that has more in common with Zionist Israel than it has with the very peoples it purports to represent! Correspondingly, there are Jews who have been drawn into this scheme and in a very odd way; they too, have become [willing] victims in this grand political and governmental overarching of regimes. The difference between the two blocs of people is that there is a minority of Jews who are in opposition to Zionism and who do not venture out to oppose the nation-state superstructure around Israel that is supportive of it. While there is a majority of Muslims who are in opposition to Zionism currently, and show every indication that sooner rather than later they will also be able to turn their attention on the larger nation-state superstructure around Israel which is working in tandem with the Zionists in Tel Aviv. The principles of justice necessitate that the whole infrastructure of injustice in the Islamic East be dismantled and discarded for once and for all.

The military fortress referred to as "Israel" has scrapped virtually all United Nations resolutions and Security Council votes against it. The Zionist divines in Tel Aviv do not answer to any *goyim* institutions; and self-righteously so, as their Zionist ideology bars them from equality, coexistence, and fairness to the other!

The Palestinians (Muslims and Christians and a small minority of Jews) have endured more than what human nature can. The horrible daily details of discrimination and prejudice, the cycles of military clampdown and wars, and the slow and gradual legal procedures that have made life a living hell for non-Jews in the Holy Land begs for a justice centered solution. Without sounding melodramatic, there remains no workable and sustainable solution to the Israeli Zionist menace except the divine justice that is outlined in the Qur'an and the Prophet's framework of social and military action.

***

The displaced Palestinian population has the right to return to their homes and homeland; and this is guaranteed to them by divine words and Scriptural justice (xxvi) .

The will to fight against oppression – Israeli style – has been fermenting now for a few generations. This will is finally finding its mode of expression in an Islamic Jihad that will bring justice to Jews, Christians, and Muslims alike.

There is always the issue bordering on paranoia that if Muslims were to remake and remodel the whole Islamic East these Jews will be once again thrown back into their historic diaspora. This need not be the case. If current Zionist- centered Jews were to abdicate their support for the Israeli nation state they would find themselves in agreement with their Islamic and Christian brethren who share in the necessity of remaking a justice centered Palestine and Islamic East. The problem will arise when some or many "Jews" begin to defend Zionist Israel as it begins its military counter-climax with the Islamic forces of liberation, justice, and equality. It will be the "Israeli/Jewish" military mobilization and its conscripts and functionaries who will risk the likelihood of finding themselves back in the international ghettoes of the world. Islamic history, with all its faults and shortcomings has never been as cruel and inhumane towards the Jewish population as other societies, especially some European ones. It would be a serious miscalculation and another human tragedy if the Zionist Jews were able to provoke Islamic justice to the extent that forces the justice-centered Muslims to be unaccommodating of Jews who want to feel at home in the Holy Land but who permit themselves to support in a passive or active sense an Israel that has proven its profanity and sacrilegious character to Muslim, Christian, and Jew alike.

Zionist Israel has managed to survive because of two sources of support: a "Jewish" bottom-up or grassroots base. These are the Jews (one third of world Jewry) who are the backbone of the Israeli regime and citizenry. The other source is an "Islamic" elite or ruling class. These are the regimes in Muslim countries that have also been active and passive in their direct and indirect support of Tel Aviv's Zionists. The Israeli official position is quickly eroding because there are Muslims for justice who can see the overall picture who are no longer fooled by false images and historical inaccuracies concerning this whole issue. *Hizbullah, Hamas,* and Islamic Jihad are the avant guard of this new wave of the future.

End Notes:

i.Indeed, [even aforetime] did We send forth Our apostles with all evidence of [this] truth; and through them We bestowed revelation from on high, and [thus gave you] a balance [wherewith to weigh social rights and wrongs], so that men might acquire a social behavior of equity... 57:25

ii.Said the great ones among his people, who gloried in their hubris: "Most certainly, O Shu'ayb, we shall expel you and your fellow-covenant-bearers from our land, unless you indeed return to our civil society." 7:88
But they who denied God['s power presence in human affairs] spoke [thus] to their prophets: "We shall most certainly expel you from our land, unless you return forthwith to our civil society." 14:13

iii. And, Lo, Moses said unto his people: "O my people! Remember the blessings which God bestowed upon you when He raised up prophets among you, and made you your own masters, and granted unto you [favors] such as He had not granted to anyone else in the world. O my people! Enter the holy land which God has promised you; but do not turn back [on your faith], for then you will be lost!"

They answered: "O Moses! Behold, furious and fiery people dwell in that land, and we will surely not enter it unless they depart therefrom; but if they depart therefrom, then, behold, we will enter it."

[Whereupon] two men from among those who feared [the power of

God, and] whom God had blessed, said: "Infiltrate upon them through the entryway – for as soon as you accede to it, behold, you shall be victorious! And in God you must place your trust if you are [truly] covenant bearers!"

[But] they said: "O Moses! Behold, never shall we move into that [land] so long as those others are in it. Go forth, then, you and your Sustainer, and fight, both of you! We, behold, shall remain here!"

Prayed [Moses]: "O my Sustainer! Of none am I master but of myself and my brother [Aaron]: draw You, then a dividing-line between us and these *iniquitous folk*!"

Answered He: "Then, verily, this [land] shall be forbidden to them for forty years, while they wander on earth, bewildered, to and fro; and sorrow you not over these *iniquitous folk*." 5:20-26.

iv.Theodor Herzl (1860-1904. Austrian Jew, founder of the Zionist movement. He was born in Budapest and became a successful playwright and journalist, mainly in Vienna. The Dreyfus case convinced him that the only solution to the problem of 'anti-Semitism' was the resettlement of the Jews in a state of their own. His book *Jewish State* 1896 launched political Zionism, and he became the first president of the World Zionist Organization 1897.

v.Arthur James Balfour, 1st Earl of Balfour 1848-1930. British Conservative politician, prime minister 1902-05 and foreign secretary 1916-19, when he issued the Balfour Declaration 1917 and was involved in peace negotiations after World War I, signing the Treaty of Versailles.

vi.Balfour Declaration letter, dated Nov 2, 1917, from the British foreign secretary A J Balfour to Lord Rothschild (chair, British Zionist Federation) stating: "HM government view with favor the establishment in Palestine of a national home for the Jewish people." It led to the occupation of Palestine and the institutionalization of Israel in 1948.

vii.Vladimir Jabotinsky (Ze'ev; 1880-1940): Writer, orator, and Zionist leader. Of Russian birth, he served as Rome correspondent for Odessa newspapers under the pen-name "Altalena," 1898-1901. Beginning his Zionist activities in Russia in 1903, he became a leading force in the scramble for what was called Jewish self-defense units, civic and minority rights, and the revival of Hebrew. In World War I, he advocated the recruiting of Jewish regiments to fight on the Palestine front; this led to the establishment of the Zion Mule Corps (1915). In 1917, the British government consented to the formation of Jewish battalions, in one of which Jabotinsky served. He organized the first Jewish 'self-defense' in Jerusalem and led it during the Arab revolt outpouring in 1920. For this he was sentenced by the British Military Tribunal to 15 years imprisonment but was soon reprieved. In 1921, Jabotinsky joined the Zionist Executive but resigned in 1923, accusing it of failing to oppose British policy with sufficient vigor. In 1925, he formed the World Union of Zionist Revisiônists in opposition to official Zionism (later also the youth organization *Berit Trumpeldor* – Betar). When the Zionist Organization coopted non-Zionists into the Jewish Agency (1929) and refused to define the aim of Zionism as a Jewish State (1931), Jabotinsky began to advocate secession; the "discipline clause," introduced in 1935 precipitated the formation by Jabotinsky of a dissident "New Zionist Organization." From 1936, he urged the speedy evacuation of East European Jewry to Palestine. Jabotinsky is considered the spiritual father and nominal head of the *Irgun Tzevai Leumi*. When World War II broke out, he again demanded a Jewish army.

[viii].*Israeli Foreign Affairs*, 4/1989

[ix].*Israeli Foreign Affairs*, 2/20/1992

[x].Marshal, J., Scott P.D, and Hunter, J., *The Iran-Contra Connection*, 1987

[xi].Jane Hunter, *Israeli Foreign Policy*, 1987

[xii].Richard H. Curtiss, *What You Won't Read About Michael Harari*, *Washington Report*, February 1, 1990

[xiii].*United Nations, Special Committee Report into Investigations of Israeli Human Rights Practices Against Palestinians and other Arabs in Occupied Territories.*

[xiv].Submitted by Giorgio Giocamelli, pursuant to the Commission on Human, United Nations

[xv].Submitted by Giorgio Giacomelli, Special Rapporteur pursuant to Commission on Human Rights, United Nations.

[xvi].Islamic Association of Palestine, 1998

[xvii].United Nations, Special Committee to Investigate Israeli Practices affecting Human Rights of Palestinian People and other Arabs of Occupied Territories.

[xviii].Ariel Sharon, Prime Minister of Israel, in an interview with General Ouze Merham, 1956.

[xix].Golda Meir, Former Israeli Prime Minister, in a statement to the

Sunday Times, June 15, 1969.

xx.Ariel Sharon, Prime Minister of Israel to Amos Oz, editor of *Davar*, Dec. 17, 1982.

xxi.Israel Wire, 1997

xxii. "O you who are committed [to God]! Be ever steadfast in upholding equity, bearing witness to the truth for the sake of God, even though it be against your own selves or your parents and kinsfolk. Whether the party concerned be rich or poor, God's claim takes precedence over [the claims of] either of them. Do not, then, follow your own desires, lest you serve from justice: for if you distort [the truth], behold, God is indeed aware of all that you do!" 4:135

xxiii. "And, withal, God does not will any oppression for His [human] subjects." 40:31

xxiv "O people! We have created you from male and female and rendered you into derivative stocks [of people] and corresponding ethnic bloodlines so that you may become familiar with each other, knowing [in the process of racial interaction] that the most honorable of you as far as God is concerned are those of you who ward off God['s corrective power in human affairs]. 49:13.

xxv "God [Himself] proffers evidence – and [so do] the angels and all who are endowed with knowledge – that there is no divine authority save Him, the Upholder of Equity: there is no divine authority save Him, the Almighty, the Truly Wise. 3:18

xxvi "God only forbids you to turn in friendly relationship towards such as fight against you because of [your civic, social, and urban expression of] faith, and drive you forth from your homelands, or aid [others] in driving you out: and as for those [from among you] who turn towards them in friendly [political and military] relations, it is they, they who are truly oppressive." 60:9

Concluding Thoughts

Since the original conference for which these papers were produced took place, a 'religious' political movement i.e. Hamas, was elected by the Palestinian people. In that context alone, it seems bizarre that we are only just starting to talk about the movement for Palestinian liberation in terms of liberationary ideas based on religion. Add to that the established practice of Christian Liberation Theology in the Holy Land (see the work of Sabeel referred to in Stephen Sizer's chapter), the calls for transformative Jewish Liberation Theology to affect that stance of Jews vis a vis the conflict (Ellis: 1987), the question of reflecting on Palestine – the Holy Land to so many – through the prism of liberation theology – seems startlingly obvious.

This volume simply presents the papers presented at the IHRC and NEDA conference on 2005. It however raises questions that need further investigation e.g. regarding the role of religion in transforming conflict into peace; the understanding of Islam in the context of struggle and liberation; the idea of being chosen within a religious context i.e. who are God's people?; can any idea of struggle based on theology eschew religious parochialism?

A few are outlined below with reference to existing projects and work in the field where appropriate. It is the hope of the book's editors that these questions are taken on board by both academics and activists in their focus on the struggle to free Palestine. As the international community has sought to undermine the democratic process in Palestine by ostracising the Hamas government, using the idea that in a post 9-11 world working with political Islam is tantamount to sleeping with the devil, it is imperative that all those involved in seeking to understand or showing solidarity with those fighting for liberation that their terms of reference are understood in their terms. Understanding does not mean accepting. However the fear of finding religious motivation acceptable in specifically Muslim or 'Islamic' terms underlies many of the narratives that seek to accommodate or tolerate Hamas and Islam as a stepping stone to some sort of society that dispenses with their presence or influence.

Add Muslims and Stir? Substituting Islam for Christianity in a Historical Discussion of Religion in Liberatory Struggle?

The papers presented have not dealt with the problematique of adopting the term liberation theology so heartily from Christian discourse. In its admitted particularism both to Christian doctrines and community and to its era, (Boff and Boff place it in terms of decades or centuries, but not trans-historically), can liberation theology be easily adapted to fit the particularities of any other religion. Ellis (1987)) elsewhere, and Ameli on these pages suggest the term's relevance but with different emphasis.

Work is already underway as part of the follow up to the conference that looks at liberation struggles in Muslim histories that draw explicitly on theological justifications. In looking beyond the 20th and 21st centuries, can we find an old way at looking at new problems?

Who is Transformed, Who is Liberated?

McVeigh on these pages sees the dilemma of Christian exceptionalism within existing theory and praxis. His own experiences highlight the application of liberation theology to a side in a conflict, in his case Catholics whose religious and ethnic identities were intertwined. Amelis' proposition that from a theological perspective, only the oppressed hold claim as God's chosen people is one that perhaps needs to pervade liberatory discourse across faiths. Ellis (1997) already highlights empathy for other struggles beyond the borders of faith. To return to the question of Palestine, is this an empathy that pervades existing practices of liberation theology. Can it be used as a principle in assessing the normative framework that a political religious movement has taken? In short should those concerned with the praxis of religion in armed conflict find a normative standard by which to judge the political and military acts of guerrillas and nascent governments?

The Right to Resist

Whilst the various movements for Palestinian liberation that have involved the use of armed struggle can call upon international law and human rights norms to support their call, is there a higher call to arms that can be invoked from a theological perspective. Whereas Jewish narratives in the Zionist context have called on a break with the past apolitical stances of Jews in diaspora in the cause of creating Israel, this narrative actually breaks the chain of the higher call as outlined by theologians in the Orthodox anti-Zionist movement (Rabkin: 2006)).

Fakhri and Ramahi allude to Islamic tenets where action is mandated by Divine imperative and apply them to modern contexts: Fakhri in the struggle to liberate Southern Lebanon and Ramahi in the context of Palestine. Again this points to the development of normative discourse outside existing human rights norms. This is a call that finds itself drawn to the debates around human rights and their universality. Whilst the secular version is now increasingly embattled, seeking a liberal communitarian trade off (see Ignatieff: 2001)), Perry and others (referred to ibid, and Perry:1998) call for a recognition of the inimitable necessity of faith as the basis for human rights. In this world view, without ultimate accountability there can be no enforcement of norms. Reflecting on Palestine, does liberation theology provide an opposite question, i.e. without ultimate authority can there be any enforcement of norms?

Transformed to What? A Universal Society of What Ends?

The fear of Islam as a state drives anti-Hamas narratives, without once seeking to establish what the norms of any such state are. As an end, is it acceptable that practitioners of any one state seek an end society where to be free is to be a member of one faith only, as Boff and Boff variously elucidate? If it is acceptable for Christians, why not Muslims, or for that matter Jews?

Is the transformed individual within a transformed society the end goal, or simply a society transformed for individuals to choose their path to individual salvation and freedom. Can the latter happen without the former? What does the nature of a transformed society through political religious liberation mean? Addressing what believers and non-believers mean by this, and not simply second guessing their ideas based on relentless demonisation, is perhaps the start of a new and old dialogue and discourse of transformation.

To seek to understand is to seek the truth. Let us pray in this case that the truth will set us all free.

Selected Bibliography

Boff L, and Boff C. (1986) Introducing Liberation Theology, Petrópolis, Orbis

Ellis, M. R. (1987) Toward a Jewish Theology of Liberation, Maryknoll, SCM Press

Ignatieff, M (2001) Human Rights as Politics and Idolatry, Princeton, Princeton University Press

Perry, M. J. (1998) The Idea of Human Rights: Four Enquiries, New York, Oxford University Press